Stags and Hens – The Remix

A comedy

Willy Russell

Samuel French — London
www.samuelfrench-london.co.uk

STAGS AND HENS – THE REMIX

Opened on 1st February 2008 at the Royal Court Theatre, Liverpool, with the following cast:

Linda	Rachel Rae
Carol	Suzanne Collins
Frances	Laura Dos Santos
Bernadette	Gillian Hardy
Maureen	Keddy Sutton
Peter	Stephen Fletcher
Robbie	Kevin Harvey
Kav	Danny O'Brien
Eddy	James Spofforth
Billy	Lenny Wood
Dave	Kris Mochrie
Roadie	Shaun Mason

The play was directed by **Bob Eaton**
Designed by **Mark Walter**

COPYRIGHT INFORMATION

(See also page ii)

This play is fully protected under the Copyright Laws of the British Commonwealth of Nations, the United States of America and all countries of the Berne and Universal Copyright Conventions.

All rights including Stage, Motion Picture, Radio, Television, Public Reading, and Translation into Foreign Languages, are strictly reserved.

No part of this publication may lawfully be reproduced in ANY form or by any means — photocopying, typescript, recording (including video-recording), manuscript, electronic, mechanical, or otherwise—or be transmitted or stored in a retrieval system, without prior permission.

Licences for amateur performances are issued subject to the understanding that it shall be made clear in all advertising matter that the audience will witness an amateur performance; that the names of the authors of the plays shall be included on all programmes; and that the integrity of the authors' work will be preserved.

The Royalty Fee is subject to contract and subject to variation at the sole discretion of Samuel French Ltd.

In theatres or halls seating four hundred or more the fee will be subject to negotiation.

In territories overseas the fee quoted above may not apply. A fee will be quoted on application to our local authorized agent, or if there is no such agent, on application to Samuel French Ltd, London.

VIDEO-RECORDING OF AMATEUR PRODUCTIONS

Please note that the copyright laws governing video-recording are extremely complex and that it should not be assumed that any play may be video-recorded for whatever purpose without first obtaining the permission of the appropriate agents. The fact that a play is published by Samuel French Ltd does not indicate that video rights are available or that Samuel French Ltd controls such rights.

COPYRIGHT MUSIC

CHARACTERS

Linda
Maureen
Bernadette
Carol
Frances
Dave
Robbie
Billy
Kav
Eddy
Peter
Roadie

SYNOPSIS OF SCENES

The action of the play takes place in the Ladies' and Gents' toilets in a Liverpool dance hall

Time: the present

ACT I Evening
ACT II Immediately after

ACT I

A Liverpool club, 1977

As the Curtain *rises, House Lights fade, Stevie Wonder's "Superstition" in all its glory is playing*

At the top of a staircase is a set of doors, which lead to the club's entrance and exit, and, centrally, a set of double doors through which we can hear music and see something of the dance floor lights seeping through from beyond. The carpeted staircase leads down to a ground floor area and the Ladies' and Gents' toilets — the interiors of which are plainly visible

Through the entrance and exit doors we see a group of girls emerge, all of them dressed in various hen night garb. They enter loudly — but beautifully — clearly enjoying themselves as they move and dance down the steps, blowing party whistles, moving and singing along to the Stevie Wonder track. At one point they naturally and effortlessly go into a unison dance sequence

Screaming with laughter they enter the Ladies', the laughter continuing as the track fades and segues to a track seeping through from the dance floor

Throughout the following the girls prepare themselves for the night ahead. Linda removes her L-plates and bride-to-be attire

Bernadette Did y' hear him — did y' fuckin' hear him?

Laughter

Carol I *saw* him – that was enough!

Laughter

Frances "How can they be so bleedin' cheesy!" he said——
Bernadette ——He said, "If I was a raindrop — I'd send you a shower."

Laughter

I said, "You can fuck off with your shower — I've got a fully fitted bathroom already!"

Laughter

Linda moves to one of the cubicles and closes the door behind her

Agh! Agh! Aren't we all havin' another great time eh? Aren't we? Aren't we, Lind'?
Linda (*from behind door*) Don't we always, Maureen?
Maureen Agh! Yeah.
Carol What about that one who came over to you, Fran, just as we were finishin' the meal?
Bernadette Oh him! Fuckin' Englebert Hump-Me-Dick!

Laughter

Frances Oh wasn't he disgustin'? He said to me, "I think you must be an engineer because every time I look at you, my nuts tighten up."

Groans and laughter

If it was up to me he wouldn't have his nuts *tightened* up — they'd be fuckin' chopped up!

Laughter

Linda (*from cubicle*) D' y' know what — that's one thing I definitely won't miss once I'm married — havin' to put up with all that kind of shite that men come out with when they're tryin' to cop with y'.
Bernadette Don't be so sure of y'self Linda? Y' think men stop bein' gobshites just 'cos you've got a weddin' ring on? If you're out an' they see you're married they think they're on — they think you're only out cos you're desperate. (*Beat*) I'm not desperate. (*Beat*) Not till it gets to about half ten!

Laughter

Maureen Agh! Aren't we all havin' another great time eh? I love it when we're all together — me, an' you, Bernie an' Carol an' Fran…
Carol (*sensing where this will lead*) Maureen!
Maureen (*tears beginning*) …an' Linda, I love Linda an' when we're all havin' another great time…

Bernadette Oh for fuck's sake — come on Mo don't start again…

Maureen …an' after tomorrow we'll never be able to all have another great time again because Linda's leavin' us, isn't she?

Bernadette (*mothering Maureen*) Come on Mo! What have we told y'? Cryin'? Y' can't cry on a night like this.

Frances It's bad luck y' know Mo, cryin' on a hen night?

Carol It is, y' know Maureen.

Maureen Is it?

Carol Yeah, if you cry on a bride's hen night it means you'll never become a bride yourself.

Maureen (*stifling her tears*) I wasn't—I wasn't really cryin' y' know Carol.

Bernadette Ah we know you weren't love, were y'? Because you are gonna make a lovely bride…one day, aren't y'? A lovely lovely bride.

Maureen D' you really think so Berni?

Bernadette Of course! Won't she girls? Won't our Mo find herself that perfect feller one of these days?

Carol (*in the mirror*) Course she will. All y' need is patience, Maureen. Some men aren't too concerned about looks.

Maureen (*beat*) What?

Bernadette (*quickly diverting; singing and banging on cubicle door*) She's gettin' married in the morning.

Others (*joining in*) Ding dong his balls are gonna shine
          Pull out his chopper
          Ooh what a whopper
          Get me to the church on time.

Maureen (*calling to cubicle*) Agh Lind', we're all so happy for y' — aren't we ?

Carol (*calling*) This time tomorrow Lind' you'll be a married woman — with your own flat, your own front door…

Maureen …your own telly, your own hoover, your own fitted bedroom… y' own husband. Agh! An' Linda's been dead lucky with Dave hasn't she…

Frances …ah he's great.

Carol …Dave's gorgeous.

Maureen He's really caring, isn't he, Dave?

Bernadette An' he's a laugh — not like the morbid bastard I married! He come in the bedroom tonight as I was getting ready — he said, "I don't know why you wear a bra, you've got nothing to put in it?" (*Beat*) I said, "Well, that's never stopped you wearin' fuckin' underpants, has it?" (*Beat*) An' I knew what he'd come upstairs for — Mr Romance — he said, "So d' y' fancy a quickie?" I said, "How would

I know the difference?"
Frances Agh! Go way Bernie — you love him really.
Carol Oh I think he's really nice, your husband.
Bernadette Nice? You wanna try livin' with him — even the kids can't stick him. "The Laxative" they call him — he irritates the shit out of them!
Frances Oh come on Berni — you've been married to him for bleedin' years — he can't be all that bad.
Carol (*to Bernadette*) An' you! You'd be moanin' about not getting' enough even if you were married to someone like — Rod Stewart!
Bernadette Oogh, what! Rod — The Throbbing Rod — Give me half the chance he could Dyno Rod my drains any day!

Laughter

Maureen Agh 'ey. We're all havin' another brilliant time aren't we — aren't we eh?
Carol Well some of us are! (*Banging on the closed cubicle door*) Come on Lind' — get a move on.
Frances What the hell y' doin' in there Linda?
Linda I'm thinkin'!
Carol } (*together*) What?
Bernadette }
Linda I'm havin' a think!
Carol Oh Linda don't start bein' stupid.
Bernadette 'Ey, 'ey, come here. (*Whispering*) Leave her, come on leave her alone — she's probably just havin' a little minute to herself.
Maureen Agh. With her thoughts. (*Beat*) In the lavvy.
Frances It's a big night, isn't it — the night before y' weddin'?
Bernadette She's probably havin' a little weep — sheddin' that last little tear while she's still a single girl.
Carol I can't wait to see her in church tomorrow.
Frances Have you seen her dress, Mo?
Maureen Oh, it's the new length, isn't it?
Frances An' what about the back?
Carol O the back's brilliant, isn't it — it hasn't got no back? Just one big plunge!
Bernadette Y' makin' it sound like somethin' y' unblock the fuckin' sink with!
Frances Oh no, it's fantastic, Berni — you wait.
Carol She's gonna look so stunnin'.
Maureen But listen — d' y' know what she said to me eh, last night? She said, "I don't even know why I'm bothering — I'd rather just get

married in a pair of jeans!"

Carol Oh when she starts all that kind of stuff y' just take no notice of her. She can be like that Linda but y' just ignore her. She doesn't mean half the stuff she comes out with.

Bernadette Oh y' mean like that, "What are y' havin' to drink Linda?" "Oh, I'll have a pint of bitter." "You will not! Not when y' out with me!"

Carol Linda just does that to be like—awkward.

Frances Yeah but she was always like—*independent*, wasn't she?

Berndette What's independent about wantin' to drink beer from a pint glass?

Maureen I'm stickin' on the brandy an' Babycham tonight — an' maybe a few vodka chasers. I wanna save myself for tomorrow.

Carol Why bother? None of the bloody fellers'll be takin' it easy, will they?

Bernadette Y'can bet they'll be pourin' it down them like there's been a drought!

Maureen Where are they havin' the stag night?

Frances Dave wouldn't tell Linda where him an' his mates were goin'.

Carol I'll bet they've gone to one of those clubs, watchin' blue movies.

Bernadette Oogh! An' here's us — just come out dancin'!

Carol Get lost Berni. Y' don't wanna be watchin' pornographic films.

Bernadette 'Ey, speak for yourself.

Maureen What are they like, Carol?

Carol Horrible. Just like lookin' in the butcher's window!

Bernadette What!

Maureen Full of chops?

Carol Blue films they're just — just — *sex*!

Bernadette Yeeees!

Carol Not sex like — like sex *should* be. When y' see a film where sex is done properly — like… like in *Emmanuelle* — well it can be lovely; soft, an' slow, in colour an' with the right music — romantic. That's how sex should be.

Bernadette That's how it *should* be Carol. But it never is love.

Carol It can be. With the right man it can. I'm not interested in fellers who want to make sex. I want a feller who makes love, not a feller who makes sex.

Maureen I just want a feller.

Beat

Bernadette Y' know when me an' my feller were still young?

Frances *Young*? Christ Berni, you're hardly an OAP.

Bernadette I know but I mean — when we still looked ahead of ourselves instead of back over our shoulders — we thought we were gonna do all kinds of things with our lives. An' what happened? I'm still comin' out — hopin' to find a bit of magic in fuckin' dumps like this.

Maureen Agh! Come on Berni.

Carol It is a hole though, this place isn't it? Why didn't we go to a proper club?

Frances Linda wanted to come here. It's her hen night, she chooses where we go.

Carol Why here though? God it's dyin' on it's arse this place.

Frances But there's a band on after the disco, isn't there? An' Linda said she wanted to dance to live music an' not just to records.

Carol I hate groups, they're never as good as the records. Why put a group on?

Frances Maybe they're tryin' to bring some life back to the place.

Carol Well I think we should've gone somewhere else

Frances Well we can do — later. But Linda wanted to come here first.

Maureen 'Ey — wouldn't it be awful if the fellers turned up here as well?

Carol Maureen don't say things like that — not even as a joke! If Linda saw Dave on the night before her weddin' it'd be awful.

Maureen I know —that's what I'm sayin' —

> "Bride and groom on wedding's eve
> Should never the other one perceive
> For if they do they'll live to see
> A marriage without harmony."
> Without harmony.

Carol That's true — it's really bad luck if you see your feller the night before you marry him.

Bernadette 'Ey — maybe that's what happened to me eh?

Maureen Ah! Did y' Berni? Did you see your husband the night before y' married him?

Bernadette Nah. Saw his best man though — spent most of my hen night shaggin' him stupid behind the Locarno.

Laughter

Come on Linda — You've gotta get ready yet.

Frances (*banging on cubicle door*) Linda! Linda, are you comin' out of there?

As they sit waiting for Linda the Lights cross-fade to the Gents'

The foyer doors swing open. Robbie, Billy and Kav are struggling to manoeuvre the legless Dave down the stairs towards the Gents'

Robbie Lift. Hold him. Lift!
Kav I *am* liftin'.
Robbie Hold the door, get the door Billy!

Billy does so and continues to hold open the door through following

Kav Lift…lift…keep him up…
Robbie In here. Let's get him in here.

They do so

Robbie Okay, put him down. Gently, gently.

As they lower Dave to the floor, Robbie now notices the vomit, which lines one of his trouser legs

(*Disbelieving groan*) Oh… No! Look at that! Fuck!

Kav and Billy see and both groan with disgust

Kav Disaster
Robbie Total fuckin' disaster for you.
Billy Y' won't get rid of a stain like that y' know Robbie. Y' see that's a puke stain. A curry puke stain. An' curried puke stain is the worst kind of stain y' get!
Robbie (*staring at Billy; witheringly*) What the fuck are y' doin', stood there?
Billy I'm holdin' the door for y' — like y' said.
Robbie (*to Billy as he enters*) But we're in now — bollock-brain! This is all your fuckin' fault gettin' everyone to go for an Indian *before* we start drinkin' instead of *after*. This is down to you!
Billy No. No, Robbie, y' see because I said we should have a curry *first* because that puts a linin' on y' stomach.
Robbie Yeh. Right! Only now it's put a linin' all down the front of my kecks as well!
Billy I didn't know Robbie. I didn't know he'd start drinking that Asti Spumante after he'd been on double Southern Comforts. Y' see, the grape an' the grain – they should never be mixed.
Robbie I'll fuckin' mix you if y' don't shut up!
Billy All right Dave? Y'll be all right now Dave. Get it all up Dave then

y' can get back on the ale!

Robbie (*taking in the state of his trousers*) Ogh! Just look at that!

Kav Major tragedy for you Robbie — fuckin' nightmare, especially when that little Bo Derek one was givin' you the eye on the way in.

Robbie Was she? *Which* one?

Billy I didn't see anyone givin' him the eye!

Robbie Fuck off you!

Kav The one by the cloakroom.

Robbie That little one?

Kav Her! Dead ringer for Bo Derek.

Robbie She was givin' me the eye?

Billy I saw her. She smiled at *me* as well y' know.

Kav Some people do react like that when they get a shock!

Robbie An' she was definitely givin' me the eye?

Kav Y' could tell she was gaggin' — she'd have been all over y' if she'd had half the chance.

Robbie Yes! Well we'll have to get out there an' give her that half a chance, won't we?

Kav I don't think so Robbie!

Robbie What? You just said she couldn't take her bleedin' eyes off me.

Kav Yeah — but that was before, wasn't it?

Robbie Before what?

Kav Before you had chicken vindaloo spewed all down y' kecks.

Billy Agh yeah — you can forget it now Robbie — you won't get a look in all night now — not when y' stinkin' like that.

Robbie That's what you think — dozy arse! (*Snatching paper towels from the dispenser*) Haven't y' heard of soap an' water? I'll have these clean in no time. (*He removes his trousers and begins to clean them at one of the basins*)

Billy I wonder where Eddy's gone.

Kav He said he was goin' the bar.

Robbie Well, he better hadn't be tryin' to chat up that lovely little Bo Derek one.

Kav No way. Eddy never wastes time chattin' women up.

Billy He always gets one when he wants one though, doesn't he ?

Kav He just waits till the end of the night, sees one an' says "Come here you!" An' they do y' know.

Billy I always go for the more "humorous" approach myself.

Robbie We've noticed!

Billy No, Robbie, girls do like to laugh! If you can "amuse" a girl then you're halfway there. Laughter is a proven aphrodisiac.

Kav Oh yeh! Fuckin' right! (*To Robbie*) I'm with him last week —

we're dancin' away with this pair an' I hear him sayin' to his one, "What's y' name?" She says, "It's Donna." He goes, "Oh! — After the kebab?"

Billy But y' could tell she was amused Kav.

Kav That's right — you just "amused" the knickers off her didn't y'? Which is why "Donna" took one look, said to her mate — "Fuck me, the martians have landed!" before the two of them grabbed their handbags an' fucked off as fast as they could!

Robbie (*drying his trousers at the wall hand-dryer*) It's all bollocks anyway — girls aren't out lookin' for a laugh — they're lookin' for a man! They're all programmed — even though they don't know it, they're all programmed to be out there lookin' for a husband — a partner, for a father to their kids — an' the secret is, gettin' to shag the arse off them before they've realized that you are not gonna be no husband!

Dave retches

Billy That's it Dave, go on — get it all up!

Kav 'Ey it's a good job his tart can't see him now, isn't it?

Robbie She wouldn't give a fuck her — she's a disgrace.

Kav She's a good laugh Linda, though, isn't she? She's all right.

Robbie I was out on a foursome with Dave an' her. Lovely little thing I was with. I get the first round in — y' know what that Linda one asked for — a pint of bitter! I'm fuckin' tellin' y — a pint of bitter! I'm out with this nice girl for the first time an' Dave's tart's actin' like a docker.

Kav She is a laugh though, isn't she?

Robbie *I* wasn't laughin. An' the fuckin' language she uses! I was fuckin' embarrassed. A woman — comin' out with language like that, I think it's a fuckin' disgrace. I said to Dave, I said I think she's well out of order. He just laughed — said she's always same but she'd soon settle down once they were married. Me? I wouldn't take the fuckin' chance.

Billy They do calm down, though, Robbie. Women — y'can't get a laugh out of them once they've turned twenty-five.

Kav (*beginning to draw on the wall*) Well, I like her — Linda.

Robbie What y' drawin' Kav?

Kav (*beginning an assured line drawing of a cityscape*) Nothin' really.

Billy (*observing as he draws*) Ogh that's dead good that. I didn't know you could do stuff like that Kav.

Kav Yeah. I used to do loads of it. Drawin' an' that.

Billy It's brilliant.

Robbie He's a good artist Kav — aren't y' Kav?

Kav (*suddenly scribbling it out*) Agh!

Billy 'Ey don't cross it out! It's dead good that.

Kav It's shite.

Billy I thought it was great.

Kav Nah. Y'shoulda seen the stuff I used to do in the Top Rank Suite.
What was that like Robbie?

Robbie Didn't y' never see that Billy? In the bogs at the Top Rank —
Kav did some fuckin' brilliant stuff in there. An' have y' never seen
what he did in the bogs at Bransky's? The whole bog wall — like a
muriel wasn't it Kav? — all fuckin' like... Town — on a wall. Next
time you're in Bransky's Billy, you go the bogs an' take a look.

Billy How do 'y' learn to draw like that Kav?

Kav I dunno. I just do it.

Billy I wish I could. I'd love to be able to draw like that — wouldn't
you Robbie?

Robbie Too right. I'd spend all day drawin' me own porno pictures.

Billy Ogh! I can do them — gis a go of y' pencil Kav. Yeh. (*He takes
the pencil and begins drawing on the wall*)

Robbie (*looking at his trousers*) Ah... Look at that. They're never gonna
dry at this rate.

Billy There's no rush anyway. We can't just leave Dave here, can we?

Robbie He'll be all right. We can keep nippin' in to have a look at him.
Where's Eddy anyway? He should be here. Dave's his best mate.

Kav Eddy doesn't like it when anyone gets pissed. He gets a cob on,
doesn't he?

Billy Eddy never gets legless himself though, does he? It's 'cos he's
captain of the team. He thinks he should set an example.

Robbie It's only Sunday League though. I mean it's not professional
football, is it?

Kav Never let Eddy hear you say that.

Robbie I'm not sayin' it isn't important — of course it's important —
it's football. It's just not *professional* football. An' sometimes — it
seems — Eddie forgets that.

Billy But that's because Eddie takes his football very seriously Robbie.

Robbie He takes *everything* seriously. I saw him laugh — once!
(*Showing his trousers to Kav*) That look all right or what?

Kav (*noncommittal*) Yeah – suppose so.

Billy Y' never gonna get that off properly with just soap an' water y'
know Robbie. Y' need petrol. Yeh.

Robbie Well I'll tell y' what... Why don't you sod off down the garage
an' get us a can!

Billy What? No, listen. If there were still petrol lighters you'd be okay wouldn't y'? It's all gas though now isn't it? See that's an example of where technology makes simultaneous gains an' losses at the same time.

Robbie Yeh that's just what I was thinkin'.

Billy No listen — see if they still had petrol lighters you'd be able to take the cotton wool out an' clean your kecks with it, wouldn't y'? Yeh. You wouldn't be stinkin' of curry then.

Robbie Yeh. I'd just be stinkin' of bleedin' petrol, wouldn't I?

Billy No, Robbie. Because it would evaporate?

Robbie I wish *you'd* evaporate! (*Noticing Billy's drawing*) What is that?

Billy It's a nudey woman. With nothin' on!

Kav She hasn't got any arms! Or legs!

Billy I know! I only do the important bits!

Robbie So where's her head?

Billy I don't do heads. I only do the important bits. I'm a primitive!

Robbie You're a fuckin' idiot. Y've given her three tits!

Billy Where?

Robbie (*pointing*) There!

Billy That's her stomach.

Kav Well why's it got a nipple on it?

Billy It's not a nipple — that's a belly button.

Kav (*bemused*) Fuck me! I'll bet Picasso's shittin' himself.

Robbie Anyway soft lad, who told you heads weren't important? The way a girl looks, her face an' that — it's dead important. There's nothin' better than a beautiful girl.

Billy They're all the same when y' get down to it though, aren't they?

Robbie Get lost. Once y' get married y' spend longer looking at them than y' do shaggin' them, don't y'? I'll tell y' la, when I get married she'll be beautiful lookin' my missus will.

Kav She might be when y' get married to her Robbie but she won't stay that way.

Robbie She will!

Kav Fuck off Robbie. Y' know what they're like round here; before they get married they look great some of them. But once they've got y' they start lettin' themselves go. After two years an' a couple of kids, what happens eh? They start leavin' the make-up off don't they, an' puttin' on a bit of weight. Before y' know where y' are the stunner you married has turned into a dog.

Eddy enters. He goes straight to the urinal

Kav What's the talent like out there Eddy?

Eddy I don't know an' I don't care. The ale's shite!

Billy Yeh, y' know why that is Eddy? Eh? It's 'cos it's pumped up with top pressure.

Eddy Oh, is that right?

Billy Yeh. I'm a real ale man I am.

Eddy Whose genius idea was it to come here? We could've stayed in the pub.

Robbie There's no talent in the pub, Eddy.

Billy CAMRA — Eddy. The Campaign for Real Ale. I've got a badge for it.

Robbie (*despairing at his attempt to clean his trousers*) Shit — this still stinks. What am I gonna do? That Bo Derek's gonna be all over me in half an hour. What's she gonna say if she can smell fuckin' curry everywhere?

Kav Tell her it's the latest aftershave.

Eddy "Madras: For Men."

Robbie 'Ey yeh... "Things happen to a feller who uses Madras for Men."

Kav Yeh. Instead of getting' y' oats y' get chicken byriani.

Robbie Curry or no curry — I'm on I am. See her givin' me the eye did y'?

Kav Yeh — it was me who told y'!

Eddy Women! Tarts!

Billy He's always on about tarts him, isn't he Eddy?

Eddy Y' know your problem Robbie — y' were born with y' brains between y' legs.

Kav and Billy laugh

Robbie That's not a problem.

Eddy Isn't it?

Robbie What's wrong with likin' the women, eh Eddy?

Eddy (*looking in at Dave*) Look at him! You'll end up like him Robbie. See him, he's the best inside player I've ever seen. But it's all over for Dave. Well, it will be after tomorrow.

Robbie Christ! Eddy, he's gettin' married, not havin' his legs sawn off.

Eddy You just watch him over the next few months. I've seen it before. Once they get married the edge goes. Before long they start missing the odd game, not turnin' up. You mark my words. The next thing is they stop playin' altogether. They have t' take the kids out on a Sunday, or they go down the club at dinnertime, drinkin'. Or they just can't get out of bed 'cos they've been on the nest all night. Nah — it's the beginnin' of the end for him.

Billy I'm not gonna get married Eddy. I'm stayin' at home with me mam.

Kav Don't you think that woman's suffered enough?

Billy I'll still be there, playin' my part in that defence, even when I'm forty, Eddy. Yeh. I keep meself fit I do.

Eddy I know y' do Billy. Y' not like Robbie, are y'? Robbie's a —"Ladies man". You'll end up like Dave, you will, Robbie.

Robbie Ah give it a rest will y' Eddy. Sunday League football isn't the be all and end all, is it? This is supposed to be a stag night, not a pre-match pep talk.

Eddy Who the fuck are you talkin' to? I'll remember that Robbie, I'll remember that when I'm pickin' this week's team.

Billy (*beat*) Are y' droppin' him Eddy?

Kav Are y' Eddy?

Robbie I don't care!

Eddy Don't y'? Not even when there's an American Scout gonna be watchin' our game?

Kav Watchin' *us* Eddy? On Sunday?

Billy I'm at the top of my form y' know Eddy. Yeh.

Kav An American scout Eddy?

Eddy There's talent scouts from America combin' this country lookin' for potential.

Kav 'Ey — we'll be without Dave. Dave won't be playin' on Sunday, will he?

Eddy That's his hard luck, isn't it? If he wants t' be on his honeymoon in Spain when we've got a scout watchin' us, that's his hard luck!

Robbie Ah come on Eddy — forget about the footie — let's get out there — listen to a few sounds, it's great when the music's playin'. Come on, have a few jars an' a laugh an' that.

Eddy snorts and turns away

Look, Eddy, I'm set up already — the dead spit of Bo Derek, isn't she Kav? Well she's bound to have a crackin' mate with her, Eddy. So I'll cop for the Bo Derek one an' you can take her mate.

Eddy Oh yeah, right. Spend all night chattin' up some woman — two hours of sufferin' her talkin', drinkin' and dancin', just to get a poke at her. Fuck off.

Billy (*at Robbie's shoulder*) I'll take her mate for y' Robbie.

Robbie Like fuck. You? The King of Comedy! I'd have to become a fuckin' celibate if I was with you. You're a sexual liability.

Billy Well. That's cos you always go after the smartest lookin' tarts in the place. I get nervous with that type.

Kav (*to Billy*) Come on. Me an' you it is. But listen — no standin' at the side of the floor all night. When I say go in, we go in — right?

Billy All right.
Robbie Come head.

The three of them move towards the door

Eddy 'Ey.

They stop

Hold on! (*Pause*) Where are you goin'?
Robbie What Eddy?
Eddy (*indicating Dave*) What about him?
Robbie What about him?
Eddy Just gonna leave him here, are y'?

The three of them, on the spot, look at each other

He's our mate, isn't he?
Kav Course he is Eddy.
Robbie Yeh.
Eddy An' you're just gonna leave him here are y'? Y' gonna leave him
  like this while y' go off listenin' to cheap music an' chasin' tarts?
Robbie Ah 'ey Eddy…
Eddy Ah 'ey what? Y' just gonna fuck off on y' mate when he's incapable,
  needs lookin' after. (*He looks at them*)
Kav He'll be all right Eddy.
Eddy That's loyalty for y', isn't it?
Robbie Well you look after him Eddy! We've had our turn. Christ we
  got him in here, didn't we? Look, me best suit — covered in vindaloo
  spew!
Eddy Haven't you heard of loyalty?

Beat. They can't move

Go on then — fuck off. I'll look after him. I'm stayin' in the bar anyway.
I'll keep nippin' in to see that Dave's all right. (*Beat*) Go on — sod
off!

They don't move

It's last out there anyway. All it is is music, fuckin' music.
Billy I like music Eddy.
Eddy You would, wouldn't y'? 'Cos you're fuckin' soft, like them! Go
  on then, get out there, an' listen to it.

Beat

Kav What's wrong with music Eddy ?
Eddy (*beat; looking at them*) Y' know what music does, don't y'?
Robbie It makes y' feel good Eddy.
Eddy Makes y' feel good! Makes y' fuckin' soft.
Robbie Come on Eddy, come with us. Dave'll be all right.
Kav There's a live group on after, Eddy.
Eddy (*turning to look into the WC*) Is there? I'll bet they're shite as well!
Robbie They're not just a local outfit Eddy. I think they've been on Top of the Pops. They'll be good.
Eddy I just saw them comin' in. I thought I recognized one of them.
Robbie Nah... That'll be from off the telly Eddy. They're big league this lot, honest.
Eddy What d' y' want me t' do Robbie? Rush off home for me autograph book?
Robbie (*to the others*) Tch — agh — come on...

They turn and go into the corridor. Eddy follows them

Kav Y' comin' then Eddy?
Eddy Am I fuck!
Billy Well where you going then Eddy?
Eddy I'm going outside — to look at the stars.

They exit from the corridor

Lights come up on the Ladies', Linda's cubicle still closed and, in each of the cubicles on either side, a pair of the other girls are standing on the lavatory from where they each gaze down on Linda

Bernadette Linda, what are y' doin' sittin' there?
Linda (*off*) I've told y' — I'm thinkin'.
Maureen Agh... (*Waving*) Hia Lind'... Agh.
Carol Are y' gonna start getting' ready Linda?
Linda (*off*) In a minute.
Carol Come on, I'll do y' make-up for y'.
Frances Are y' all right Lind'?
Bernadette You'll have to get a move on Linda — all the good lookin' lads'll be gone if they think I'm not showin' up.
Maureen (*producing a quarter bottle of vodka*) Lind' — d' y' wanna drink? (*Reaching to offer down the bottle*) Linda — I love you y'

know. An' tomorrow — I am gonna be the — *best* — Linda, the *best* — bridesmaid — that a bride could ever wish for — because *you* — Linda — are the best bride that a best bridesmaid could ever be a best bridesmaid for — an' I mean that, Linda — I mean that from — the bottom——

Bernadette (*relieving her of the bottle and leading her out of the cubicle*) —from the bottom of the half bottle of voddy that you've been swiggin' on the sly since we come out.

Maureen Berni! I haven't been doin' nothin' on the sly!

Carol Come off it — you? You could peel a fuckin' orange in y' pocket you could!

Maureen (*affronted*) I've only been havin' a little drink Carol! To calm my nerves. (*Beat*) I am a bridesmaid you know!

Bernadette Yes! An' carry on drinkin' at this rate you'll be a fuckin' horizontal one. Now come on Maureen! You're not even ready yet.

Frances Are you gonna do your zip up Mo?

They watch as Maureen ineffectually tries to zip up the front of the dress

Maureen I think this dress must have shrunk a bit.

Bernadette Of course it has love.

Carol Either that or some little piggie's been at the pies again!

Bernadette Carol! (*Helping Maureen*)

Others follow suit

Come here.

Frances Let's see.

Carol Breathe in! Hold y' breath.

Bernadette It's no good. Lie her down. Lie down.

Frances On your back Mo.

Maureen lies flat on her back, allowing the zip to finally be pulled up by the others

Bernadette (*turning back to the mirror with the others*) There y' go Mo. (*She makes last minute make-up adjustments*)

Carol Have y' bought a weddin' present Berni?

Bernadette Course. (*Sotto voce*) We've got them a coffee table — in antique!

Un-noticed by the others, Maureen is now so tightly zipped into her dress that she is unable to get back on to her feet

Carol Ah that's great — we've got them a coffee set.

Bernadette What about you Fran — what have you and Tony got them?

Frances (*beat*) Him? I'm not with him any more. (*She shrugs*) We split up last month.

Bernadette God you'd been goin' with him for ages.

Frances I know — but I started to realize we were incompatible. Well I was a Sagittarius, wasn't I? An' he was a twat.

Becoming aware of prostrate Maureen, they lift her back onto her feet

So their weddin' present's just from me. I hope it's all right — I've got them a coffee percolator.

Maureen Ah Fran — of course it's all right — that's a lovely present because everybody knows that a coffee percolator turns a house — into a home.

Bernadette I just hope to fuck they like coffee!

Maureen Ah they will do Berni — because that's what y'do when you become a couple; you might drink tea when you're at home with y' mum but when you become a couple you drink coffee. Agh — that's worked out brilliant, hasn't it? Because now, when their friends come round they'll be able to make coffee in Frankie's percolator, drink it out of Carol's coffee cups, sittin' at Berni's antique coffee table, eatin' my coffee liqueurs. Agh — they'll be like a coffee co-ordinated couple, won't they?

Bernadette Fuck!

Her dress and make-up complete, surveying herself in the mirror

God! I'm gorgeous! Come here, here (*Pulling the others in front of the "mirror" and forming a "tableau"*) Look at that. Look at that — power! (*Beat*) Minge on mass! (*She leads them in screaming, part- scandalized laughter before going over and knocking sharply on the cubicle door*)

Maureen Agh aren't we all havin' another great time.

Bernadette (*calling*) Linda, Linda!

As they wait for her, the Lights cross-fade to the Gents'

Robbie and Billy burst through the double doors and into the Gents'

Robbie The bitch… the stuck-up bitch…

Billy (*quickly checking on Dave*) Y' all right Dave? Okay mate?

Robbie Snotty cow! She was dead fuckin' humpety anyway! The gob on her!

Billy An' what did she say to y' Robbie?

Robbie I've told you three times, haven't I? What d' y' want me t' do, write it out for y'?

Billy No, but I couldn't hear y' in there, with the music an' that... Go on, what did she say?

Robbie Cow! (*Beat*) "I never dance," she said, "with men in suits!"

Billy Is that what she said?

Robbie A suit? What the fuck's wrong with a suit? I thought she must be jokin' at first, y' know, comin' on with the laughs an' that. I give her this fuckin' killer smile an' said to her, "I'll tell y' what babe, if you don't like suits why don't we go back t' your place — where you can take it off for me."

Billy Did y'? What did she say then?

Robbie (*beat*) She fuckin' walked away from me. A *suit*? What's wrong with a suit? Hepworths, this come from — *Hepworths*. There's no rubbish goes on my back.

Billy I know Robbie — you're very particular — sartorially, aren't y'?

Robbie Fuckin' weirdo she was — lucky escape there. An' once y' got in close she didn't look like Bo Derek at all – she looked more like fuckin' Bo *Diddley*! I told her, though, y' know. I caught up with her at the bar, I put her straight – I said, "Listen love, I'd buy y' a drink but I wouldn't waste my time on a tart who doesn't know quality when she sees it."

Billy Is that what you said Robbie?

Robbie Too right...! "This suit, this suit", I said, "cost the best part of a hundred notes!" See the boat race on her then when I told her that?

Billy Yeh! Robbie. An' then she said "You were robbed."

Robbie I thought you said you couldn't hear!

Eddy enters the corridor

Billy Not what you said Robbie. But I could hear her.

Robbie Well y'wanna get y' fuckin' ears washed out don't y' cos she never said that.

Billy She did, Robbie, I was standin'...

Eddy enters the Gents'

Robbie All right, Eddy. We were just keepin' an eye on Dave for y'.

Eddy Good lad.

Robbie Doin' y' a favour.

Eddy Yeh... Kav's doin' the same for you out there!

Robbie What?

Eddy Know that one who keeps givin' you the elbow, the one who looks like Bo Derek — She's dancin' with Kav. She's all over him.

Robbie I don't care! I wasn't interested anyway... She's just a fuckin' waste of make-up!

Eddy laughs at Robbie who heads for the door

Come on.

Eddy (*as Robbie and Billy leave*) Go on then — go on — piss off. Sod off t' y' dancin'. An' y' music. Fuckin' music makes me wanna throw up! Hey Dave — is that what made you spew up eh? Music! (*He produces a quarter bottle of Scotch and removes cap*)

The Lights come up in the Ladies'. The WC door opens. Linda stands in the doorframe

Linda "But if we do not change, tomorrow has no place for us."

Beat. The other girls are stood looking at her

Carol Are you all right ?

Linda That's what it says — on the wall, in there.

Bernadette Oh! they must have had one of them student nights here.

Carol Who else would write shite like that?

Bernadette Students! They've got more bloody brains than sense. Wouldn't you think — with all that education they could write somethin' sensible on the toilet wall?

Linda Come on... Let's go.

Carol Go where?

Linda Out there.

Frances Linda, you haven't done y' make-up.

Carol What about your hair?

Linda I can't be arsed. Come on.

Bernadette You are not goin' out on that dance floor without y' make-up an' your hair done.

Linda Why not?

Maureen Ah, Lind' — It's your hen night. You wanna look your best on y' hen night, don't y'?

Frances Don't worry, we'll wait for y' Linda.

Bernadette Are y' getting' a bit nervous love?

Maureen Agh, are y' getting' the butterflies for tomorrow Lind'?

Bernadette We know, love, we know what it must be like for y' — but we're your mates Linda — we're not gonna let y' do anything stupid.

So come on, get that make-up done.

Linda Why? It doesn't matter!

Maureen Oh God Lind' — I'd feel naked goin' out there without any make-up. D' y' know, I was dead late for work once an' I rushed out the house forgettin' to put my eye shadow an' mazzie on. An' all the way to work I felt dead weird without knowin' why — I kept thinkin' I'd come out without puttin' any knickers on. But when I got to work an' looked in the mirror I saw it was my eye shadow an mazzie that was missin' — that's what was makin' me feel so undressed. I had to borrow some make-up from Pauline Golightly — shot the bathroom an' lashed some on. An' I was fine then. It was only when I was walkin' back across the yard I realized — I didn't have any knickers on! So that shows y' doesn't it?

The others, including Linda, laugh

Linda (*relenting; opening her bag*) Oh for Christ's sake — go on, I'll do my make-up, I'll see y' out there.

Carol Linda, we're your mates, aren't we? Y' don't think we'd desert y' on your hen night, do y'?

Linda You're not deserting me. I'll come an' find y' when I'm ready.

Bernadette We'll go out when we're *all* ready.

Carol That's us — we always stick together, don't we?

Linda Why don't y' all come on my honeymoon as well?

Bernadette We would Linda love, but I'm afraid if I was there, you wouldn't get a look in.

Linda Look… I am a big girl now y'know. I can find me way out of the Ladies' an' onto a dance floor.

Bernadette Linda — it's your hen night, we stick with you.

Linda Y' mean until some feller wants to take you outside, Berni? Then you'll be off like a flash.

Bernadette Well — a girl's got to have a bit of fresh air now and then, hasn't she?

Linda Oh is that what you call it — fresh air?

Bernadette Listen love — with some of them, that's all it feels like!

Carol What are you like! Does your husband know what you get up to?

Bernadette He doesn't care! I was comin' out tonight, he said, "what time will you be in?" I said, "well, if I'm not in bed by midnight, I'll come home!" (*She laughs*)

Linda Well you'd better watch out tonight, Berni. You're might have a bit of competition.

Bernadette Ooh! From who? Not… The-Bride-To-Be?

Linda Why not? It's my last fling, isn't it?

Jeers from the others

Frances If you don't get a move on, Linda, your last fling'll soon be flung! Come here. (*Taking comb and beginning to do Linda's hair*) Go on, you lot — there's no point all of us waitin' round.
Carol Yeh, come on, we'll get the drinks in.
Frances Get us a Bacardi an lime.
Linda Get me a pint of lager will y' Berni?
Bernadette Linda, no! This is a hen night — not a stag night.
Linda All right, I'll have a pint of mild!
Bernadette Linda!
Linda Well all right, get me a fuckin' snowball! In a *ladies'* glass, with a lovely little cherry on the top.
Maureen Ah — I think I'll start with one of them as well Lind'.
Bernadette Come on. We'll see y' in the bar. Come on girls… (*She sings "That's The Way" as she leaves the Ladies'*)

Maureen and Carol follow Bernadette, also join in with the song

Linda (*sigh*) Jesus, what're they like!
Frances And you, what's wrong with you tonight?
Linda Nothin' it's just… Oh come on, hurry up, I wanna get out there an' just — get lost in it.
Frances Music?
Linda Yeh.
Frances It's great the way it gets to y', isn't it — music?
Linda Like you can come out sometimes an' feel really shitty, can't y'? — But as soon as you walk into that music — bang; it's like everything changes.
Frances It makes y' feel special doesn't it?
Linda (*beat*; *sigh*) I get lost in music. I become someone else.
Frances Yeh I'm like that.
Linda D' y' know if it wasn't for music — I wouldn't be getting' married tomorrow.
Frances Oh Linda!
Linda Fran — I'm tellin' the truth. Me an Dave were dancin' this slowy *When A Man Loves A Woman* it was. I heard this voice whisperin' in my ear, like it was part of the music, sayin', "will you marry me?" So I said yeh. (*Beat*) But I think it was the music. I think I might have said "yeh" if I'd been dancin' with Frankenstein.
Frances Linda don't be stupid.

Linda When the music ended I looked up an' there was Dave, beamin' down at me, talkin' about gettin' married — an' I'm wonderin' what he's on about! Then I remembered. And the next thing y' know, I'm here, tonight — an' tomorrow I'll be married.

Frances Are you tellin' me you're havin' second thoughts?

Linda (*beat*) Oh come on — that'll have to do — I just wanna get out there an' dance myself stupid. After tonight I might never have the opportunity again.

Frances For God's sake, Linda — you're gettin' married, not gettin' locked up!

Linda (*making a final check in mirror*) Y' do get frightened though, y' know. I mean if it was just gettin' married to Dave it'd be okay — he's all right Dave is. But it's like, honest, it's like I'm getting' married to an entire bleedin' town.

Frances A *town*?

Linda It's like — I marry Dave... I marry everything else at the same time. Like, I could sit down now an' draw you a chart of everythin' that'll happen to me after tomorrow.

Frances D' y' know something Linda? You're my best mate, but sometimes — you don't half talk shite.

Linda (*laughing*) I know, I know, I know. An' you just keep tellin' me Fran.

As they exit

An' do you know what I keep tellin' myself? Well, at least after tomorrow I'll be the proud owner of my own hoover, my own telly, my own front room — an' more fuckin' coffee beans than they've got in Brazil!

The pair of them laughing as they exit

The Lights come up in the Gents', Eddy is taking a swig from the quarter of Scotch

Eddy Hey, Dave... D' you wanna drink, Dave? (*Laughing*) Can't y' hear me Dave? Jesus! You wouldn't hear if a bomb went off would y'? But that's your own fault Dave. Y' can't blame me. Y' don't *have* to drink do y'. See, y' don't have to do anythin'. (*Beat*) The US, Dave, the US of A! An' you could've been alongside me... You should've been comin' with me. Not with a wife though. Y' can't travel when there's too much baggage weighin' y' down. (*Beat*) She's okay... I suppose, your one... Linda. She's all right. But round here Dave —

get married an' you're fuckin' trapped! Y' don't go anywhere after that. Just stay forever in this dyin' dump. It's hard to get out as it is Dave you know that. Look at all the talent scouts who've seen our team. But I'm still here, aren't I, eh? Even when you've got talent it's still no guarantee that you'll make it. But once y' get married... There's not even a fuckin' chance of makin' it then! Baggage! No baggage — so that when the chance does come along — you can be off, away, out of it. (*Beat*) Like me, Dave — that's why I keep myself — free. Anywhere! I can go anywhere, anytime! There's nothin' holdin' me back. (*Beat*) But if you don't wanna come with me, Dave — if you wanna get married to some tart, well you — just fuckin' do it. Yeh you do it!

Robbie and Billy enter the foyer area and go down towards the Gents'

Eddy goes to take a swig from the bottle

Robbie and Billy enter

Eddy quickly hides the bottle in his pocket. Billy stands at the door. Robbie goes to the urinal

Robbie All right Eddy. (*Seeing Billy holding the door*) Come in an' close the bleedin' door will y'?

Billy What have we come in here for? We told those two we'd see them in the bar.

Robbie Yeh — soft lad — we told them that 'cos we wanted t' get rid of them, didn't we?

Billy Did we? Mine was nice!

Robbie Nice? I thought there'd been a fuckin' breakout at the zoo — shoulda seen her Eddy!

Eddy Where's Kav?

Robbie What?

Billy We saw him goin' out the back Eddy — with that one who looks like Derek someone.

Robbie I hope he gets a dose.

Eddy (*moving to the door*) I'm goin' the bar. Soft gets...

Billy Are you pissed Eddy?

Eddy (*wheeling and grabbing him*) Have you *ever* seen me pissed?

Billy No Eddy.

Eddy No Eddy... I don't get pissed. I'm not like you. I'm not like him... I don't get pissed.

Billy No Eddy, what I meant was ——
Robbie Billy — shut up.
Eddy Yeh, you shut it. Soft arse! (*Pushing him away and going to the door*) Look after Dave. I'm goin' the bar.

Eddy goes into the corridor and exits

Billy I think he might be a bit pissed y' know Robbie.
Robbie Well, there's no need to go tellin' him, is there? He thinks he never gets pissed. But I've seen him in a state loads of times.
Billy Well, why doesn't he just say, y' know, that he's pissed?
Robbie I don't know, do I? He just likes to pretend, y' go along with him don't y'? It's like he pretends that one day he's gonna play big league football. Y' just go along with him.

Kav enters. Sheepish

Kav I'm sorry Robbie.
Robbie (*all innocence*) About what Kav? What's up?
Kav Y' know.
Robbie What? What?
Kav Me coppin' off — with that little Bo Derek one. I'm sorry Robbie. It wasn't my fault though, honest, because she was——
Robbie Whoa whoa, hold on — the Bo Derek one? Did you hear that, Billy?
Kav What? What's wrong?
Robbie Ah no — you'll be all right — as long as y' didn't nip outside with her.
Kav I did! Round the back.
Robbie Yeh, but y' didn't slip her one, did y'?
Kav You're jokin' — she couldn't wait.
Robbie Kav, Kav!
Kav What's up?
Robbie Come on Kav. Why d' y' think I knocked her back?
Kav You?
Robbie Yeh! 'Cos Stevie Thomas told me, didn't he? He nabbed me in the bar and warned me... That one who looks like Bo Diddley? He copped a dose off her last month! She's got the clap! Come on Billy — those two'll be up in the bar now. Ogh — wanna see these two we've tapped off with Kav, stunners. What they like, Billy?
Billy Y' should see them Kav. Ugliest pair of boots y' ever saw in y'——
Robbie Go way soft lad — take no notice of him, he's blind.

A coughing from the WC alerts them over to Dave

Go on Dave — get it up.

Billy It might be a gold clock, Dave.

Kav Don't y' think we better get him sobered up? It is his stag night, isn't it?

Robbie You're considerate all of a sudden, aren't y'? I'll bet y' weren't thinkin' of Dave an' his stag night when y' were round the back gettin' a dose off Bo Diddley.

Kav I haven't got a dose. You were just messin'.

Robbie You wait an' see pal. You wait.

Kav Go away. Come on... Let's try an' make him get it all up.

Robbie Ah leave him. Christ it's not a proper stag night if the groom's conscious.

Billy It's bad luck if the groom's sober the night before he gets married, yeh.

Robbie That's right that is. My dad told me. He was sober on his stag night an' look what happened to him the next day!

Kav What?

Robbie He married my mother! All right, come on. Just get him back over the bowl an' he'll be okay.

Peter enters from dance floor doors. Passing him, carrying gear is the Roadie

Peter Have y' cracked it?

Roadie (*non Liverpool*) Have we fuck. Every socket I try just blows. What y' doin' out here?

Peter Lookin' for a loo — there's none workin' backstage.

Roadie Some gig this is — the place should be condemned — along with the whole fuckin' city if y' ask me.

Peter Hey bollocks! It's my hometown you're talkin' about!

Roadie Yeh — an' now I can see why y' left it!

The Roadie exits

Peter goes into the Gents' and to the urinal, looking back over his shoulder at the activity in the cubicle

Peter He's in a bit of a state, isn't he?

They look at Peter

What's up with him, one over the eight?

Robbie No, it's his hobby, lookin' down bogs!

Peter (*laughing*) No accountin' for taste eh?

They stand and look at Peter. Peter zips up and returns the gaze

Kav Do you get paid to look like that?

Peter (*laughing*) Yeh! I suppose I do.

Robbie Look at the fuckin' boots!

Peter Good, aren't they? (*Showing them off*) Like them?

Billy They look like tarts' boots to me.

Peter They are "tarts" boots. Good though, aren't they?

Robbie Good?

Billy I wouldn't even wear shoes like that if I *was* a tart!

Peter walks past them and takes a closer look at Dave

Peter What's he been drinkin'?

Robbie Y' what?

Peter Are you deaf?

Robbie What the fuck is to you what he's been drinkin'?

Peter It's one of *my* hobbies, getting' to know what people drink.

Billy He was on erm, Black Velvets to start with but then he went on the Southern Comfort — an' that was before we had couple of bottles of Asti Spumante in the Indian.

Peter Oh, right. That type is he? Subtle palate?

Kav Listen you — who the fuck d' y' think you're talkin' to?

Peter Kavanagh, isn't it? Erm… Tony Kavanagh.

Kav How the fuck d' you know my name? How does he know my name? Listen you, you just… (*Pointing*) Hold on — 'ey — it is, isn't it? It is! You used to live round our way, didn't y'?

Robbie Ogh fuck. It's *you*, isn't it?

Peter I hope so.

Billy *Who* is it?

Kav You know — him! With the… He's in the group er hold on, hold on, don't tell me… It's erm — erm.

Peter Peter…

Kav That's it, that's… Peter McGeegan.

Robbie Fuckin' hell — you're famous, aren't y'? Is it your group — that's on tonight?

Kav 'Ey… I always said you were dead good on the guitar, didn't I, Robbie? Here, look, that's Robbie. Y' remember Robbie, don't y'?

Peter Erm — yeh — hi.

Robbie (*handshaking*) Put it there mate — all right Peter. Love the boots.
Billy *Who* is it?
Kav An' Billy... Y' remember Billy, don't y'? Billy Blake?
Peter Erm...h
Kav Ah y' do... Y' must do... His mam an' your mam were mates...
  Remember...
Peter Oh yeh... All right erm...

*As Peter shakes his hand, Billy doesn't know whether to bow, curtsey or
wind up his watch*

Billy *Who* is he?
Kav Look at you now! Jeez. An' you used to be just like us! Hey! Look
  who's here. (*Leading Peter to WC*) It's Dave! Y' remember Dave,
  don't y'?
Peter Er, I don't think erm... I
Kav Ah y' do. You remember Dave. (*Shouting*) 'Ey Dave, Dave, wake
  up... Look who's here Dave! Dave — come on. Wake up.
Peter It's okay, look leave him it doesn't...
Kav Ah Dave'll be dead sick at missin' y'.
Peter Maybe that's the best thing eh?
Kav (*laughing too much*) Still kept your sense of humour eh? Great.
Robbie So what are you doin' playin' in a dive like this?
Peter Well, it's work, isn't it?
Robbie You've been on the telly, haven't y'?
Peter Yeh, a couple of times, yeh.
Robbie An' the radio.
Peter Yeh.
Robbie So why come back to play in a dump like this.
Peter It was just a — bookin' y' know. I think it was arranged before
  the single happened.
Robbie But y' still come back an' played it? Nice one Peter, nice one
  mate.
Billy (sotto voce *to Robbie*) Who — is — he?
Robbie Live in London now do y'?
Peter Yeh.
Kav Give us a piece of paper, who's got some paper?
Robbie What's it like?
Peter Y' know — yeh, it's — okay.
Robbie I'll bet it's fuckin' — brilliant!
Peter It's all right.
Robbie Jesus!
Peter Small world eh?

Kav (*coming out of the WC with toilet paper and pencil*) Sorry about the
  erm, I couldn't find any other paper… (*He offers pencil and paper*)
Peter Ah come on, you don't need to…
Kav Could y' put — "To Kav – an old mate".
Peter Look man, for God's sake you don't want me to do this…
Kav You're jokin', aren't y'? Of course I do…
Peter Come on — we went to the same school for Christ's sake.
Kav I know. I'm gonna show that to everyone.

*Billy comes out of the WC with a piece of paper, joins the queue. Peter
signs*

Robbie 'Ey is it true what they say about the — y' know, the groupies?
Peter Most of it's fiction.
Robbie Ah you're just sayin' that. I bet you can have anythin' y' want,
  can't y'?
Kav (*admiring the autographed sheet of loo roll*) Look at that!

Peter takes Billy's paper and signs it

Robbie What sort of a car d' y' drive?
Peter Do you know, I don't. Listen, what you lads doin' these days?
Robbie Fuck all, us. So do you have your own driver?
Kav Have y' got your own house in London?
Peter A flat. So — what, none of you are workin'?
Kav Yeah, we all work.
Peter What sort of work's that then?
Kav Just fuckin' borin' — you wouldn't wanna know. Go on, tell us
  about, y' know, what it's like…
Robbie Have you ever met the Rolling Stones?
Peter (*laughing*) No!
Robbie Haven't y'?
Kav Who then? Go on — who's the most famous person you've ever
  met?
Peter Listen, come on, you don't want…
Billy (*has been studying his autographed sheet of loo roll*) Who is he?
Robbie Can't you fuckin' read!
Kav Leo Sayer — have you ever met Leo Sayer?
Peter (*balking at the preposterousness*) No!
Robbie So like, of everyone you've met — go on — the *most famous*.
Peter Well — erm — I suppose — it'd have to be… Elvis.
Robbie Fuckin' hell! You've met Presley?
Peter *Costello*!

Neither Robbie or Kav have the first idea of who he's talking about

Robbie Who?
Peter Elvis Costello? (*Forcing himself*) An' erm, when we recorded the
Top of the Pops thing we er — erm, — Rolf Harris was on as well.
Robbie (*instant awe*) Rolf Harris? Kav — Kav!
Kav You have met Rolf Harris? Hey, hey… (*He offers his hand*)
Robbie Rolf is Kav's hero.
Billy Can you guess what it is yet?

Billy approaches Peter and offers his hand, which Peter dutifully shakes.
Billy stands looking proudly at his hand

Robbie (*taking up position*) Kav! Kav!

Kav and Robbie go into their Kangaroo Down, Sport routine. Peter can
only watch — and suffer

Peter (*finally feeling able to*) Listen lads — great to see y' but I've gotta
— we haven't even got the gear set up yet.
Robbie Aren't y' gonna come an' have a bevy with us?
Peter We haven't even sound-checked yet.
Kav What about afterwards, y' know after the gig?
Peter Yeh, maybe — that's — yeh a possibility. Yeh. Anyway I've
gotta, y' know, tune up an'… Hey, look after the Southern Comfort
King won't y'?

Lads laugh as Peter exits to corridor, the lads follow him to the door

Kav Comfort King… Listen, see y' Peter — see y' later.
Peter Yeh, see y' lads.
Robbie Hey — Break a leg Peter.

They watch as Peter disappears before they move back inside the
Gents'

Kav Isn't that just — amazin' — Peter McGeegan!
Robbie Been on Top of the Pops — an' he still comes back to play a
dive like this.
Kav But these are his roots y' see Robbie. An' he's not the kind of feller
who'd forget somethin' like that.
Robbie I would! See me comin' back to play dumps like this if I'd been
on Top of the Pops!

Kav Did y' see his boots?

Robbie Fuckin' brilliant.

Billy I'm gonna get a pair of them.

Robbie They wouldn't look the same on you.

Billy Why not?

Robbie Because it's not just the boots — is it? It's the way you carry them off.

Kav An' they'll be custom made — boots like that.

Robbie Christ — the way he must live eh? I'll bet he's never bored is he?

Eddy enters

Kav Eddy… Eddy guess what?

Robbie Wait'll we tell y' Eddy.

Kav Guess who's here tonight?

Eddy I know! Dave's tart!

Billy ⎫   ⎧ Who?
Robbie ⎬ (*together*) ⎨ What?
Kav   ⎭   ⎩ Linda?

Eddy I've just seen her now, out there — dancin'!

"Superstition" snap to full volume

Black-out

ACT II

Bernadette, Frances and Carol make their way into the Ladies';
laughing

Bernadette Did y' see the size of him? He was all of four foot fuck-all
— I didn't even know he was dancin' with me till I looked down an
spotted him — I nearly fuckin' stood on him! He's stood there with a
big soft grin on his face like one of the seven fuckin' dwarfs.
Frances Him an' his mate — they were like shingles — y' couldn't get
rid of them!
Carol An' they wouldn't take no for an answer. I said to the spotty
one. God! He was horrible. I said, "I'll let you into a secret — you're
wastin' your time tryin' it on with me — because I'm a lesbian!" Ogh!
He said, "I love a challenge!"
Bernadette The little midget one, he's (*demonstrating*) givin' it all that
gyratin' groin like he's got somethin' down there — St Vitus fuckin'
dance if y' ask me. He's still got this dozy grin on his gob — I said
what's wrong with you. He said, "Nothin' babe — just showin' my
appreciation for such a fine specimen of the more mature woman."
Little twat!

Others laughing

I'm just about to swat the little bastard with my handbag an' he goes,
"Y' know somethin' doll — play your cards right an' you could be
goin' down on me later!"

Laughter

I said, "Listen, y' little germ — go down on you? I'd rather go down
on the fuckin' Titanic!"

Laughter

Linda and a now very well-oiled Maureen "dancing" their way to the
Ladies', giving it loads and accompanying themselves with the cho-
rus/riff of Stewart's "D'ya Think I'm Sexy"

They enter the Ladies' arm in arm and still singing, the others take up the chorus until they're all singing

Above it all we hear:

Maureen Ah — aren't we all having' a fabulous time eh? Aren't we all...

Others joining in — affectionately taking the piss

Maureen ⎫
Bernadette ⎬ (*together*) Havin' another great time!
Frances ⎬
Carol ⎭

Maureen Ah, we are though, aren't we?

Linda I love *this*. I love it when we're all out an' together an' it's just — *us* havin' a laugh an' a dance...

Maureen An' a drink! I've had a lovely little drink y' know.

Linda (*embracing her*) We know you have, sweetheart. An' that's why I came an' rescued you from that short-arsed little runt.

Bernadette You an' all? He tried it on with you Maureen?

Maureen He wasn't too bad — at first y' know... Mm. I was dancin' with him an' he said to me, "D' y' wanna come back to my place?" I said, "What for?" He said, "For a fuck and a pizza."

Others laughing

I said, "Is it a wholemeal pizza?"

Others laughing

An'— an' he must have thought he was on then — because he said, "Come the bar an' I'll get y' a drink." Well, I thought — I like a little drink — don't I?... So I went with him an' he said, "So, what y' havin" I said, "I'll erm — I'll have a triple pernod — an' ice!" He said, "On y' bike! Y' can have half a lager an' like it!" An' then he said, he said, "I'm not fuckin' made of money y' know." An' so I said, (*beginning to laugh*) an' I was dead made up with this — I said, "Listen, you! To make you out of money — it'd only cost about three an' a half pence."

Laughter

He got dead narked then — said he was — fed up cos people had been takin' the piss all night just because he wasn't the tallest person in the room. I said to him, "Well — you wouldn't even be the tallest person in the room — if everybody else was lyin' down…" But I think that hurt his feelings an' I felt a bit sorry for him then. So, I said, "Well — y' could do something; to cheer y'self up couldn't y'?" He looked all hopeful again then. "Oh yeh?" he said, "An' what did you have in mind then, doll?" I said, "Well y' could go'n have a nice swim, couldn't y'? — In your fuckin' half a lager!

Laughter

We're havin' a good time, aren't we? Aren't we eh? We're all havin' another good time. Linda — Linda, are you havin' a good time?

Linda I'm havin' a *brilliant* time Maureen.

Frances God, can't y' tell she is? She hasn't stopped dancin' since she got out there…

Linda Come on, let's get back out there. An' we'll just dance together — us.

Maureen Just the girls dancin' together — no men.

Carol We'll have a line out.

Linda An' if any fellers try to split us up we'll tell them where to get off.

Maureen (*cueing – they've done this before*) Because…

Linda ⎫
Maureen ⎬ (*together*) … because. Because.

All Because… (*singing "We Are Family" and dancing their way out of Ladies' and along corridor*)

The Lights come up in the Gents'. The fellers are all as at the end of ACT I

Eddy Talk about a fuckin' rope round y' neck… She's not even married yet an' she's keepin' tabs on him!

Kav Yeh, but what I'm tryin' to tell y' Eddy is…

Eddy It's his stag night, isn't it? Couldn't she just leave him to his mates on his last night of freedom?

Kav Eddy…

Robbie She won't know Dave's here, Eddy. She'll only be here for a dance.

Kav Eddy guess —

Eddy Dancin'! Oh yeh, she's dancin' all right. I just seen her from the balcony, with all different fellers, the bitch!

Robbie Come on Eddy, the girl's only dancin'.

Eddy Oh is she? An' what about him? (*Dave*)

Kav Eddy forget that… Listen, y' know who's been here eh? Guess! —

who's been standin' on that very spot you're standin' on?

Billy Y' should've seen his boots Eddy. Custom-made, y' know — hand-tooled.

Kav Go on Eddy, guess, guess who?

Eddy I don't know, do I?

Kav Peter McGeegan!

Eddy Who?

Kav Peter McGeegan, Eddy. Remember? He used to live round our way, played the guitar. This is his group that's on tonight. They're really gettin' famous Eddy.

Eddy Famous?

Billy He knows Rolf Harris, Eddy!

Kav You'll be able to meet Peter yourself, Eddy. We're all gonna have a drink with him — y' know, after the gig.

Eddy After the *what*?

Kav That's what they call it when they play somewhere, Eddy — the "gig".

Eddy The — *gig*!

Kav Yeh

Eddy I thought you were supposed to be lookin' after Dave.

Billy We have been, Eddy.

Robbie (*to Dave*) All right Dave? Okay mate?

Billy Feelin' a bit better Dave?

Kav It was great just meetin' him y' know Eddy. He's not a bit stuck up or anythin'. (*Bringing out his autograph*) Look Ed.

Eddy takes it

See, it says, "To Kav — an old mate". An' that's his signature.

Billy He did one for me Eddy, look. Yeh.

Eddy takes it and looks at it

I'll bet he'll do one for you Eddy, if y' ask him.

Eddy What's this?

Billy Yeh, it's dead hard to read at first Eddy, but look it says…

Eddy *This*? Fuckin' scraps of paper!

Kav We didn't have an autograph book with us Eddy.

Eddy What are y'? Little fuckin' kids?

Kav What?

Eddy *Kids* get autographs. Is that what you are — little kids?

Kav No Eddy, but it's Peter McGeegan — he's becomin' really famous!

Eddy Famous! Fuck off! (*Crumpling the paper in his fist*) Famous! (*He* *goes to the WC, throws the paper down the pan and flushes it*)

Kav Eddy! What have y' done?
Eddy What have I done?
Robbie You've just flushed Dave's head, Eddy!
Eddy Good! Do it again. It might sober him up.
Kav Eddy! That was my autograph!
Billy An' mine. But y' couldn't read it anyway!
Kav That was my fuckin' autograph!
Eddy (*swiftly grabbing Kav*) Who the fuck d' y' think you're talking to?
   (*He glares him into submission*) Y' don't get autographs from people
   like him! He's just a fuckin' no-mark!

He glares at Kav who stares back, helpless. Eddy finally pushes him away

You don't wanna waste y' time Kav. See, it's people like you Kav,
runnin' around after pricks like him — that's what makes them
what they are. You're as good as he is! But did he ask you for your
autograph? Did he?
Kav (*quietly*) No.
Eddy No! You wanna keep hold of your dignity you do, Kav. You're
as good as him. You could do that, what he does if you wanted to.
You can do anythin'. We all can. We can do anythin' we want to do,
anythin'. He's nothin' special, so don't you belittle y'self beggin' for a
scrawlin' on a piece of bog paper. We can all write our names y' know.
Here, here, give me that pen. Give it me!

Kav does so

Look, look it's dead easy y' know. You want an autograph? I'll give y'
a fuckin' autograph... Here.

Eddy writes his name on the wall

Kav It was great meetin' him though. Wasn't it Robbie?
Robbie It was all right. (*Beat*) I suppose.
Billy Gis a go of the pen Eddy... I'm gonna do my autograph. I am. I'm
gonna do mine bigger than yours Eddy. Yeh.
Robbie He's nothin' special, is he? Hasn't even got a fuckin' car. (*Writing
his name*) Y' shoulda seen the stupid boots he had on Eddy, y' know,
women's boots. (*Taking out a felt-tipped pen and adding his own name*)
He's no one really — anyone could do what he does.
Kav Oh! yeh. Anyone could do it, Robbie. An' that's why — later on,

whilst he's stood up on the stage with all the coloured spotlights on him, you'll be down on the floor, just like the rest of us dancin' through the dark with all the other nomarks.

Eddy (*angrily snatching the felt-tip from Robbie*) Give me that. (*To Kav*) Put your name up there.

Kav What for?

Eddy Put y' name up.

Kav (*beat*) I don't wanna put my name up.

Eddy Why not?

Kav There's no point, is there?

Eddy The *point* is that our names are up there. Where's yours?

Kav shrugs

It's got t' be there.

Kav Why?

Eddy So that all our names can be seen, that's why. So that everyone'll know we've been here.

Kav They'll only paint it out. They always do.

Eddy Let them, we'll come back an' do it again.

Kav Then they'll stipple over the walls with artex so y' can't write on them.

Eddy So. We'll come back *again*. An' the next time we'll *carve* our names. We can do anythin' Kav. (*Beat*) Now. Write y' name.

Robbie Go on Kav. I wouldn't mind, but you can write better than any of us.

Eddy Come on Kav. I want y' t' do it for me. Y' know the way y' do it in fancy scrolls an' that, that's clever that is Kav. You do it. For us, for y' mates — come on.

Kav eventually looks at the wall and the names written there

Kav Who taught you lot how to write? That's fuckin' terrible that.

Eddy You show us how it should be done Kav.

Kav reaches out and take the felt-tipped pen

Good lad. Good lad, Kav.

Kav Go on, you'se lot go. It'll take a bit of time this. Go on, I don't mind keepin' my eye on Dave, Eddy.

Eddy Come on...

Eddy goes out and up the steps followed by Robbie and Billy

Robbie Y' gonna get out on the floor then Eddy?
Eddy No way.
Billy Why not Eddy?
Eddy 'Cos I'd rather just sit an' watch you'se make dickheads of yourselves.

They exit

As Kav continues writing his name in ornate script, Bernadette and Carol followed by Maureen, come through the doors, down the steps and into the Ladies'

Bernadette The thoughtless, inconsiderate bastards!
Maureen What is it? What's wrong?
Carol They must have known!
Maureen What!?
Bernadette How much have you had to drink?
Carol Are you sayin' you didn't see them?
Maureen Who?
Bernadette Dave's mates!
Carol Robbie Smith an' Billy Blake — they're here — tonight.
Maureen Oh I like him, Billy Blake — he's nice, isn't he?
Bernadette But Maureen, love — if Billy Blake an' Robbie Smith are here, then who else must be here?
Maureen (*beat*) Oh my God! Oh no — the bridegroom, Dave! Where's Linda, get Linda…
Carol (*restraining her*) Frances is lookin' for her...
Maureen If they bump into each other!... "Bride and groom on wedding's eve. Must never the other one perceive. For if they…"
Bernadette Maureen! (*Beat*) They're not going to bump into each other.
Maureen (*beginning to be tearful*) But y' never know Berni an' if they did it'd be one almighty disaster because the bride and groom can't see each other the night before — they just *can't* Berni.
Bernadette Which is why, Maureen, we're gonna wait in here till Frances brings Linda back so that we can safely get her out of this place an' then go on somewhere else.
Carol I was dead made up at first — when I saw Robbie Smith — he's well fit, him.
Bernadette Fit or not — we've got a responsibility to make sure Linda does not see her intended tonight.
Carol Do y' still think it really matters — all that stuff ? Some couples just ignore it these days.
Maureen Yes, Carol — like my Auntie Jean! The night before her

wedding she an' her intended went the bingo together! Everyone
warned her but she took no notice — her an' her husband-to-be sat
there, side by side in the Mecca, the pair of them chasin' a full house
on the eve of their weddin'. Three months after they were married —
what happened? He got run over by an articulated fish van on Speke
Boulevard! My Aunty Jean never got over it. To this day she still can't
even look at a piece of haddock. Says if she ever gets married again
she'll go the bingo on her own.

Frances hurriedly walks along corridor closely followed by Linda

Linda Frankie, for God's sake what's goin' on — what's wrong?

Frances Just hurry up — come on, quick. (*Holding open the door to
the Ladies'*) In here.

Linda (*as they enter the Ladies'*) It better be worth it — I came here to
dance not to jangle all night in the bloody Ladies'!

Bernadette (*seeing Linda and Frances enter*) Carol — you go get the
coats!

Maureen Did y' see anyone Frankie?

Frances No, it was all clear.

Maureen Oh thank God!

Carol Cloakroom tickets — come on, give us your tickets.

Linda What's goin' on?

Bernadette Linda, we've got to get out of here!

Linda Says who? I'm enjoyin' myself.

Maureen So was my Auntie Jean, Linda! But she'll never eat haddock
again!

Linda What!?

Bernadette Linda, Dave's here!

Linda Dave?

Maureen *Here*, Lind'. With Billy Blake an' that lot.

Linda Dave never said he was comin' here.

Bernadette Well, he has Linda — an' that's why we've got to get you
out of here.

Linda Why?

Maureen "Bride and groom on wedding's eve. Should not..."

Linda (*laughing*) Oh for God's sake Maureen — don't talk shite!
(*Continuing to laugh before realizing that everyone around her is
unamused*) Oh come on!

Bernadette Linda — it's not our fault that the lads turned up here.

Linda Or mine. But sod them! What difference does it make to us?

Bernadette If Dave wasn't with them it wouldn't make a scrap of
difference — but Dave is with them!

Carol Your bridegroom Linda.

Linda So?

Bernadette Oh Linda, don't start!

Linda Don't start what?

Bernadette Bein' miss awkward arse!

Linda I'm not bein' awkw——

Frances —But it is bad luck Linda — we're only thinkin' about you.

Linda All right — well if you're thinkin' about me let's just like — stop this fuckin' nonsense about movin' on somewhere else. Let's just go back to havin' a good time.

Bernadette Oh yeh! An' how are we supposed to have a good time when we can all see that you're puttin' the future of your marriage in jeopardy!?

Linda (*beat*) Okay, look, right, okay. So, you've all told me that if I stay here I'll be takin' some awful risk.

Maureen Linda — is one night of bingo worth a lifetime of loneliness?

Linda You've warned me — an' I understand — if I'm gonna risk years of bad luck then I've got no one blame but myself. Okay? But that's a risk — I — am going to take.

Beat

Bernadette Oh no you're not Linda.

Carol We're your mates.

Frances So we're not just gonna stand by an' watch as you do something stupid!

Maureen (*tearful*) We're only thinkin' about you Linda, because we love you.

Bernadette (*comforting her*) It's all right Mo, come on love.

Carol (*indicating Maureen*) See! See what you're doin'?!

Linda Me!?

Bernadette (*comforting Maureen*) Come on love, don't cry.

Maureen (*sobbing*) I just — want — everything to — be nice!

Linda Oh for fucks sake!

Frances I know you're my best mate Linda — but sometimes you can't half be an awkward cow!

Beat. As Linda looks at them all, they are all looking at her

Linda I love bein' out with you lot. (*Beat*) But sometimes — you just turn into this — *thing!* An then you make me sick! (*Beat*) Because you never do what you want to do. Just what you're told.

Bernadette Nobody tells me what to do Linda!

Linda No? All right. You came here tonight to look for a feller. Well there's hundreds out there. So come on — come an' get yourself one.

Bernadette Oh I could do Linda — easily. But for your sake I'm——

Linda —Forget about *my* sake will y'?

Bernadette I can't Linda — because unlike you, I care about what happens to my mates.

Linda (*beat*) I'm goin' back out. (*Opening door and holding it*) Who's comin' with me ?

They make no move

Well sod y' then! (*She turns and goes out*)

It appears as if Linda is headed back to the dance floor. However, she comes to a halt and props herself against the wall, banging her head against it in frustration — this happens throughout the following

Bernadette Well if you ask me I say she's not been herself all night.

Frances But that's what she's like Berni. How long have I been her mate eh? An' I've seen her — she can be like this.

Bernadette It's not just that Frankie — it's the pressure, love. I mean she might be acting all calm and cool — but she's under a lot of strain.

Maureen They say, don't they Berni — "A woman on the verge of marriage — is a woman on the verge of insanity!"

Carol What are we gonna do?

Maureen If she's in this kind of state now, just imagine what she'll be like tomorrow.

Frances Look — what I think we should do is go an' see the fellers. Tell them that they'll have to move on somewhere else.

Carol Yeh but will they though?

Bernadette They'll have to.

Frances I'll go an' see Eddy Ainsworth.

Bernadette Oh is he here?

Frances Yeh. An' if he tells them to leave they will.

Frances exits to the corridor. Lights fade in the Ladies'

Linda (*as Frances passes her*) Frankie…

Frances (*with attitude*) What!

Linda (*beat*) Oh forget it.

Frances Listen Linda — I don't know what's wrong with you tonight but you can't half be an awkward bitch.

Linda turns away

Frances goes on her way and exits as Peter and the Roadie enter

Roadie The circuit board's lethal. If this doesn't work then I don't know what the fuck I'm gonna do — apart from shovin' the gear back into the van an' just gettin' out of here.
Peter Without playing at all?

Linda looks up in recognition

Roadie Well if I can't get any power what else can y' do? I mean its...
Peter All right, all right all right. I don't...
Linda My God!
Roadie (*thinking it's him whom she's addressing*) Oh all right sweetheart — how y' doin'?
Linda (*passing him*) McGeegan!
Peter Come here, you. (*He embraces her*)
Roadie (*continuing on his way*) Fuck!

As they drop the embrace, stand back and look at each other

Linda Look at the state of you!
Peter What d' y' mean?
Roadie (*calling*) Hey — McGeegan, don't forget you're on in a few minutes.
Peter I thought you couldn't get any power.
Roadie I will now!

The Roadie exits

Linda (*shaking her head as she takes in his appearance*) What happened to you?
Peter What *didn't* happen to you?
Linda Don't start!
Peter Me?
Linda Yeh! (*Shaking her head and laughing again; Beat*) So how long have you been with this lot then?
Peter We formed just after I got to London. (*Beat*) Did you know we were playin' here tonight?
Linda No.
Peter What — you just out for a dance?
Linda Yeh — sort of.

Peter I'd have thought you'd have given up comin' to this kind of place by now.
Linda Oh, would you? Well what I do — or don't do — is no concern of yours!
Peter How long is it since we last — met?
Linda I dunno. (*She does*; *beat*)
Peter A long time?
Linda Yeh.
Peter So don't you think we could — observe a bit of a truce! Start again? (*He looks*)

She shrugs

Hello Linda. It's nice to see you again. You look really lovely.
Linda Oh fuck off!
Peter Come here.

They embrace – laughing as they do

Frances appears in corridor

Frances clocks them as Linda pulls away from the embrace. Frances pulls open the door to the Ladies' and, once it's closed, leans back on it

Peter Isn't that... What's she called, your friend?
Linda Frankie — Frances.
Peter Frankie, that's right. How is she?
Linda She's all right.
Peter (*beat*) It really is great to see you y' know.
Linda It's great to see you. I suppose.
Peter I'll go an tune up if y' like — say tarar now!
Linda Go on then.
Peter (*beat*) So you don't fancy a dance then?
Linda With you?
Peter Well — in the absence of — John Travolta — yeh, me!
Linda (*beat*) Okay.

They begin to move along corridor

Do you think you'll be *able* to dance — wearing boots like that?
Peter Do you like them ?
Linda Where the hell did you get them from?
Peter There's this brilliant shop, just beyond Chelsea — fantastic gear

— you'd love it. It's *Exit* mostly imported stuff, some second-hand but all of it really...

They go through the doors

Frances pushes herself away from the outer door and through the inner door to the Ladies'

Bernadette Well?
Frances What?
Bernadette The fellers!
Carol Are they gonna move on somewhere else?
Frances No. No, they're stayin' here they said.
Bernadette The selfish bastards!
Frances It doesn't matter anyway.
Carol Apart from the fact that we've gotta find somewhere else to go now.
Frances I think it might be too late anyway,
Maureen Oh God, oh God — has she seen Dave already?
Frances No, not Dave. You know there's a group on here tonight? Guess *whose* group.
Bernadette What?
Frances Peter McGeegan — it's his group.
Carol They're never as good as the records — groups.
Bernadette Peter who?
Frances McGeegan — yeh. Linda's ex.
Maureen Oh my God.
Carol He's here tonight?
Frances They're right outside there, top of the stairs — all over each other!

Maureen emits a wailing cry and heads for the sanctuary of a cubicle from where subsequent cries punctuate what follows

Bernadette Well the little bitch! That explains everythin' doesn't it?
Carol I wondered why she was so keen to come to a dump like this!
Frances Hold on — we can't be sure that she knew who——
Bernadette —Oh come off it Frankie.
Carol How long was she goin' with him?
Frances A couple of years.
Carol If she went out with him for that long she's bound to know what he's up to these days.
Bernadette There's bloody big posters outside — she must've known

he was playin' here tonight.

Carol Fancy pullin'a stunt like that the night before your weddin'.

Maureen (*tearful; from a cubicle*) An' we were all havin' such a good time, weren't we?

Frances Look, hold on, she might have just been y' know — for old times sake.

Carol You don't do that — arrange to see an ex, the night before you get married.

Frances We don't know that she did that. She might just have bumped into him, mightn't she?

Bernadette Well, we can soon find out, can't we? Out there — she's out there? Right! (*She exits the Ladies' to the corridor*)

Maureen (*from a cubicle*) Why can't everythin' just be nice?

Carol I knew all along we shouldn't have come here. We could've gone the Top Rank Suite!

Bernadette enters the Ladies'

Bernadette Where did you say they were?

Frances Just outside there.

Bernadette Well they're not there now!…

Carol Well where've they gone?

Bernadette You tell me, Carol — you tell me. But it doesn't take a genius to work out that that girl is playing with fire.

Cries from the cubicle

Now we're her mates — and it's our responsibility to make sure that that girl doesn't get burnt.

Maureen (*crying*) Everything was so lovely and now it's not lovely at all!

Carol For Christ's sake Maureen will y' give it a bleedin' rest!

Maureen (*from the cubicle*) I only want things to be nice!

Bernadette (*going to the cubicle door*) Who said things won't be nice Mo?

Maureen It's gonna be my Auntie Jean all over again an' I don't know if I can take much more!

Bernadette Maureen, we're going to sort it out! Don't you worry — everything will be nice, Maureen. There's a wedding tomorrow. And there'll be a nice cake and a nice service, nice bridesmaids, nice presents. And a nice bride with a nice groom. And everything will be fuckin' nice! But Mo, we've just got to make sure that Linda doesn't do anythin' silly because of this — mood that she's in. We're her mates Mo — an' we've got to look after Linda — in her hour of need. That's what mates are for, isn't it Mo? Now come on, open this door. Come on Maureen.

Maureen comes out of the WC and Bernadette puts her arm around her, leading her out

Don't you worry love — everything will be nice. We'll see to that. Now come on.

The girls go into the corridor

Billy and Robbie coming through the corridor doors

Robbie All right girls?
Bernadette (*shepherding them along the corridor*) Come on girls.
Carol (*stopping*) Hia Robbie.
Robbie All right erm — "Carol" isn't it?
Carol (*flattered*) You're good at names, aren't y'?
Robbie I'm good at most things Carol.
Carol Have y' seen me dancin'? I mean really dancin'.
Bernadette Carol!
Carol See y' then Robbie. Might see y' at the weddin' tomorrow.

She dashes off through the doors, following the others

Billy You're on there y' know Robbie.
Robbie Yeh. Don't really fancy it though.
Billy Don't y'?
Robbie Nah. I'd shag it though! But come on, if we don't get back those other two might do a bunk. They're well fuckin' fit those two aren't they?
Billy Yours is Robbie.
Robbie She looks dead like… Whats-her-name… Olivia Newton John — doesn't she?

As they enter the Gents', the Lights come up

Billy Yeah.

In the Gents', Kav is putting the finishing touches to an impressive pictorial representation of his name

Robbie Agh – look at that!

Billy That's brilliant that, Kav.

Kav It's all right, isn't it?

Robbie S' great. 'Ey Kav, y' wanna see this lovely pair we've copped off with — mine looks just like Olivia Newton John — doesn't she Billy?

Billy Yeh! Mine looks just like *Elton* John!

Robbie Agh stop y' moanin' you! She's all right.

Billy That's dead smart that is Kav.

Robbie Don't even think about doin' a bunk on your one because if you give her the elbow it means I'm knackered with my one.

Billy But I don't like her Robbie.

Robbie Why not ?

Billy I just don't! She's got no — like — personality.

Robbie (*beat*) She's got a pulse, hasn't she!

Billy I think it's important — personality.

Robbie Ah come on Billy, stop bein' an arlarse. All right, so she's not like, the best cracker in the box. But she's all right. An' I'd do the same for you — if it was the other way round — I'd do the same for you Billy.

Billy Would y'?

Robbie You know I would Billy. Because I'm your mate — aren't I, eh? Eh?

Billy Yeh.

Robbie An' you're my mate. (*Beat*) An' a mate is someone y' can ask for a favour. That's what I'm askin' you Billy.

Kav He's right y' know, Billy. Stand by your mates an' they stand by you.

Maureen, Carol and Frances come down the steps and into the Ladies', followed by Bernadette

Billy Go on then, Robbie.

Robbie Agh, good lad Billy — I knew you wouldn't let me down. Come on, let's get out there. Hey — it's smart that is Kav. Eddy'll be made up with that.

Kav (*following Billy and Robbie as they exit*) Yeh, I'm gonna show him.

Bernadette enters the Ladies'

Bernadette Well the brazen cow!

Carol I could barely believe my eyes.

Bernadette *Dancin'* with him! She looked like she was stuck to him!

Frances An' ignored us — just bleedin' ignored us!
Bernadette I don't know if she even saw us — as far as I'm concerned there's only one thing that she's got her eye on tonight!
Maureen What Berni?
Carol Oh come on Maureen — you saw the pair of them!

Linda comes through corridor doors, headed towards the Ladies'

Bernadette You don't dance together like that unless you've got just one thing in mind.
Maureen What? What?
Bernadette Don't make me spell it out Maureen — I'm upset enough as it is. I think she's — disgustin! The night before her weddin'! I mean, if you ask me there's...

Linda enters the Ladies'. Silence as Linda walks past them and into a cubicle, closing door behind her

Bernadette (*clearing throat*) Linda... Linda.
Linda (*off*) Yeh?
Bernadette Don't you think, Linda, that you're bein' just a touch — insensitive? Even, inconsiderate, Linda.
Linda (*off*) How's that Berni?
Bernadette (*beat*) Well — do you think it's right — carryin' on like this with a stranger, the night before your weddin'? D' you think that's right?
Linda (*off*) He's not a stranger. He's someone I happen to know very well. In fact, Berni, you could call him an intimate friend!
Bernadette (*rapping on loo door*) Don't you try an' take the piss out of me Linda!

Cubicle door opens and Linda emerges

Linda Berni! I'm dancin' with him — that's all. (*She crosses to a basin*)
Carol But y' don't deny you used to go with him!
Linda No! An' why should I deny it?
Carol Well, don't you think that makes it a bit rich? Carryin' on like that with an ex?
Linda I don't think it makes it anythin'. An' for your information, I'm not *carryin' on* with anything or anyone. I'm dancin' with him! Dancin' with someone I happen to like — like very much in fact. An' I think that's got sod all to do with you or you or you or any of you!
Bernadette An' have you forgotten that tomorrow you and Dave will

be stood in a church where you will become man and wife?

Linda (*finishing drying her hands before going to door*) An' what makes you think I'm still goin' through with it?

Beyond the door, and where it can't be seen by the others, we see the smile on Linda's face before she exits

Maureen (*heading for a cubicle*) Ogh — this is makin' me ill — I'm gonna be sick.

Carol I'm supposed to be a bridesmaid an' everythin'.

Maureen (*off*) What are we gonna do? (*Appearing at the cubicle door*) What are we gonna do — with all the coffee equipment?

Bernadette This is getting' out of hand this is.

Frances What can we do Berni?

Bernadette Y' know who's to blame for all this? That Peter Mc... What's his name?

Carol But what can we do about it Berni?

Bernadette Well, for a start, Carol — the sooner she gets away from that Peter feller the sooner she'll start comin' to her bleedin' senses.

Frances She is makin' such a fool of herself.

Bernadette She's makin' a fool of everyone. (*Beat*) Well I think we better let the fellers know about this.

Bernadette makes her way into corridor, followed by the others

Frances Oh! we can't drop her in it with Dave.

Bernadette We won't bloody *need* to drop her in it, will we? If she keeps flauntin' herself out there he'll soon see it for himself, won't he? Come on — let's see if we can find Eddy Ainsworth.

Maureen What are y' gonna say to him Berni?

Bernadette I'm gonna tell him what she told us — that the weddin's off!

As they exit, Peter and Linda enter – as if from the bandroom

Linda So that means you won't be playin'?

Peter Doesn't look like it. Every time they connect to a socket it just blows. The place is fallin' to bits.

Linda It's like everything else round here. The place is dyin'.

Peter Maybe that's why I was surprised to see you still here. I thought you'd have left by now.

Linda An' gone where?

Peter Anywhere. I just never thought you'd stay round here.

Linda An' what's wrong with "round here"?

Peter Come on! You just said yourself — the place is dyin'.

Linda So?

Peter So — maybe you're right an' that's why you should think about movin' on.

Linda (*beat*) What d' y' think gives you the right come out with things like that!

Peter Linda! It was *you* who said it.

Linda Yeh! An' I can say that! I can say just what the fuck I like — about livin' here because, I do *live here*.

Peter Oh! An' because I no longer live here I can't have an opinion about the place.

Linda That's right!

Peter Don't you think that's just — a little unreasonable?

Linda Yeh — I think it's totally outrageous! But it's how it is Peter. So when you come back here an you hear one of us slaggin' off the place — don't think it gives you the right to join in. You left! Remember?

Peter Yeh! — An' all I'm sayin' is, you should've come too. When I went to London — you should have come with me.

Linda I couldn't, could I?

Peter *Wouldn't*

Linda All right — wouldn't.

Peter Why?

Linda (*beat*) Because — I didn't — love you enough. (*Beat*) I didn't half like you a lot though.

Beat

Peter So what are y' gonna do then? Settle down here?

Linda I might.

Peter An' what about bein' happy Linda?

Linda I am happy.

Peter Are you? Happy like you always said you dreamed of bein' happy. Or happy like you used to say wasn't happy at all — was just — slowly dyin', with a smile.

Linda Oh fuck off, you! Just cos you went to bleedin' London. We do know where it is y' know — London. I mean it's only two and a half hours away on the train. Christ you'd think you'd gone to the other end of the world to hear you talk. It's only a train ride away.

Peter Not when you've only got a single ticket.

Linda Comin' back here, tellin' everyone what to do!

Peter I'm not tellin' you what to do.

Linda You think y' can — You think y' can tell everyone what to do —

just because you can get away with wearin' women's boots!

Peter I'm not tellin' you anythin' Linda. You do whatever you like — stay around here. Have y' kids an' keep y' mates an' go out dancin' an' go the pub an' go the shops an' do all those things — that you used to tell me you hated doin'.

Beat

Linda I was dead young then. An' you do hate all those kind of things when you're young.

Beat

Peter An' how old are you now?
Linda You don't know?
Peter Twenty-two. In June. Right?

She nods

Twenty-two! An' already you're in trainin' to be a fuckin' geriatric! (*He watches, awaiting her reaction*)

Linda Thanks for remindin' me what a real bastard you can be!
Peter I know I am — a selfish, shitty bastard because I did what I wanted to do. I did the worst thing possible — I got out.
Linda An' just because you did y' think everyone should do the same.
Peter No — but I think you should!
Linda Why?
Peter Come on Lin'. Because you want to. Because while you're doin' all this number you hate it. You do it — but while y' do it you hate it.
Linda I don't hate anything about my life! I love doin' what I do.
Peter Like — bein' out with y' mates?
Linda Don't you dare slag my mates. I love my mates — all of them.
Peter Yeh?
Linda Yeh.
Peter So how come you're out here with me an' not with them?
Linda What? Y' think cos of you?
Peter No. Not because of me. But because you know — right inside there (*heart*) that you want out!
Linda Do y' know somethin'? I didn't think you could get more fuckin' arrogant than you already were.
Peter I'm right though, aren't I?
Linda No! Just so arrogant that you *think* you're right — about everything.

Beat

Peter Once we've finished here tonight, we're in the van and away. Scotland tomorrow night, Newcastle on Sunday, day off Monday then on to Norwich, Southampton, a couple more dates on the south coast. Then back to London.
Linda So?
Peter Come with us.
Linda Peter — I gave you your answer a couple of years ago.
Peter Yeh — but then I was askin' you to come with *me*. This time, lovely, I'm just offerin' you a lift. You can get off wherever you want.
Linda I never accept lifts off strange men.
Peter Yeh. Because that might involve taking some kind of a fucking risk, mightn't it?
Linda Oh — God speaks does he!? Listen, Mr bleedin' know-all — it'd be great wouldn't it — me speedin' through Scotland with some second-rate band when there's two hundred family and friends stood in a church tomorrow waitin' to see me get married!

Beat

Peter We are *not* a second-rate band! (*Laughing*) No messin'?
Linda Why do you think I'm here tonight? It's my Hen Night.
Peter (*laughing*) *Hen* night! Jeeesus. D' y' want us to play "Congratulations" or "Get Me to the Church on Time"?
Linda Neither. Just give us a kiss.

They kiss and embrace before Linda pulls back, looks at him and then hugs him before breaking away and moving towards the doors leading to the Ladies'

Thanks for lettin' me have me last fling with you. (*She turns to go*)
Peter Hey! D' y' love him?
Linda Accordin' to my mates I do.
Peter Lin' — do you?
Linda What's it to you Peter?
Peter I'm just tryin' to understand why you're stayin'.
Linda Don't you ever listen? I told y' — I'm gettin' married tomorrow.
Peter But that isn't what I asked y'?
Linda (*smiling at him*) Tara Peter.

Linda descends steps to the Ladies'. Peter stares after her for a moment before turning and making his way down towards the Gents'

In the Ladies', Linda goes into a cubicle

In the Gents', Peter, seeing Kav's handiwork, stops to look at the drawing. The doors to the dance floor suddenly burst open as Eddy, Robbie, Billy and Kav pile though the doors and down the steps

Robbie An' so the weddin's off, is it Eddy?

Eddy You're jokin' aren't y'? She might fuckin' say it's off. But no one makes a laughin' stock of my mate.

Billy Too bleedin' right!

Eddy Thinks she's some kind of clever tart, does she? Well we'll soon sort her out! An' that fancy fuck she's been dancin' with!

Robbie The fuckin' cheek of him though — comin' up here an' nabbin' Dave's tart! Thinks he can just come here an' take whatever he likes.

Eddy He'll think again when we've finished with him.

Eddy throwing open the door to the Gents' and marching in followed by the others. Peter looks around from the drawing

Peter All right lads?

Eddy All right? All — right? No it's fuckin' not all right!

Peter Well?

Eddy You what!? You just fuckin' shut it! (*Beat*) Are you a tart?

Peter looks back, sighs

Hey! I asked you a question.

Peter No! I'm not — a tart.

Eddy Well why y' wearin' tarts' boots?

Beat

Peter Because I like them.

Eddy Well I don't!

Peter No — well...

Eddy I don't like you either.

Peter No. Well, yeh. I'd gathered that.

Eddy Oh, you had — had you?

Peter Well...

Eddy You've been dancin' with our mate's tart.

Peter (*suddenly shocked*) What!

Robbie His fiancé! — while Dave's lyin' in there — with a stomach complaint!

Peter Hold on! Look, I didn't know she was anythin' to do with...
Eddy You've been fuckin' about with our mate's future missus.
Peter Hey, look — hold on!
Eddy No! You just fuckin' hold on. Comin' back here — poncin' an'
posin' around the place — like y' think y' can just walk all over us.
Peter I don't think anythin' of the kind I just...
Eddy As if you're somethin'— *special*. As if you can do all kinds of
fuckin' things that we can't? Well I'll show you — oh I'll fuckin'
show you what we can do.

*Eddy suddenly lunges forward and grabs Peter, propelling him towards
the urinal as if he's going to smash his head into the wall. Stopping
before the wall, however, Eddy holds Peter's head so that he's forced to
stare at Kav's drawing*

That's — what we can do! Look! Fuckin' look!
Peter I *am* lookin'!
Eddy Well look again! Because we did that!
Billy Yeh, Eddy but more Kav than anyone Ed, it's...
Eddy (*releasing his grip on Peter and turning on Billy*) Shut the fuck
up!!!!
Robbie (*to Peter; of the drawing*) That's clever that is!
Peter It is — I agree.
Eddy Oh! Do you?
Peter (*to Kav*) Is it yours?
Kav What!
Peter Did you draw it?
Kav (*shrugs*) It's nothin', is it?
Peter It's clever — skilled.
Eddy Anythin'! We can do anythin'!
Peter Did you ever consider goin' to art school?
Robbie (*laughing*) Art school? Listen to the stupid get!
Eddy (*laughing*) Hey Kav, Kav — you could be an artist you could.
(*Laughing*) Look out — here comes Picasso Kavanagh.
Robbie (*camping*) Oooh — can I hold y' brush for y', duckie?

Eddy, Billy and Robbie are laughing

Kav (*joining the laughter*) Art school, me? The only kind of artist I
wanna be is a piss artist.

Laughter

Peter You sad bastard!

Eddy leaps on him, grabbing and pinning him down

Eddy Don't you *dare* — don't you fuckin' dare. You, y' piece of shit —
comin' round here — with y' *music* — fuckin' music, makin' people
unhappy! Now you listen — you go anywhere near Dave's tart again
tonight an' you are fuckin' dead!
Peter Okay! Okay! Okay!
Eddy She belongs to him — in there, our mate. An' we look after our
mates we do. We stick with them. You left this town. You walked out.
You've got no claims here. You left! So when you've finished tonight
you just fuck off out of it — take y' music an y' tarts boots back to
whatever shit hole they come from!

He propels Peter towards the door and finally through it

Now do one!
Billy (*shouting after him*) An' don't come back y' big poufter!

*As Peter makes his way up the stairs, Linda emerges from the cubicle
and goes to the basin*

Eddy Right! That's him sorted. Now let's go an' see Dave's tart!

*As they leave the Gents', Bernadette and other girls are approaching
the Ladies'*

On the upper level, the Roadie enters

Peter comes face to face with Roadie at top of steps

Roadie Peter, it's no good mate — I've tried every power source…
Peter Forget it! Let's get the gear in the van and piss off out of here.

They exit

Bernadette and the girls come face to face with Eddy and co.

Bernadette We can't find her anywhere Eddy.
Eddy We will!

The fellers exit. The Lights fade in the Gents'

The ladies continue on their way to the Ladies'

Bernadette (*watching Eddy and co make their way up the stairs*) Ooh
— I wish you'd find me Eddy!
Carol D' y' fancy him?
Bernadette Rotten! Ooh!

They enter the Ladies'

Linda What y' doin' here?
Bernadette (*aside to Maureen*) Go tell Eddy she's in here.

Maureen exits the Ladies' and goes up the steps

Linda I thought you'd be out on the floor Berni — there's not a lot of
single fellers left y' know.
Bernadette I hope you are thoroughly ashamed of y'self.
Linda Oh Christ Berni — leave it out, it doesn't matter. Come on...
Bernadette It doesn't matter!? You just listen to me for a minute.
Linda (*standing to attention*) Yes Miss!
Carol Well don't listen Linda — carry on ignorin' your mates.
Bernadette An' bein' a selfish bitch!
Linda (*making the effort – deep breath*) All right. Okay. Go on — I'm
listenin'.
Bernadette I've been married, Linda, for some years now. You're
forgettin' that I've already been through what's happenin' to you. An'
I understand, Linda, I do.
Linda Okay.
Bernadette D' you think you're the first woman to have a few doubts
the night before she gets married?
Linda Berni — you don't have to worry because...
Bernadette Don't interrupt me Linda! Every woman has doubts. But
that's all they are — doubts. Y' don't act on feelings like that. Just
because y' feel a bit nervous about everythin' doesn't mean y' can go
rushin' into the arms of some ex-boyfriend an' then disappear with
him...
Linda (*warning*) Berni!
Bernadette What would happen if every other woman did the same
thing an' acted on her feelings? Who the bleedin' hell would *ever* get
married if we all took notice of how we feel?
Linda Berni — am I allowed to speak now? Can I get a word in? (*She
looks at them – the intensity causing her to suddenly laugh*)

Eddy and the others come charging down the steps

Robbie Eddy... Eddy — don't be daft — we can't go in there...
Carol See! See what she's like!
Linda Carol, look — all of y' — for your information, you can all stop
worryin' because I've got no intention of...
Eddy (*pushing open the door of the Ladies' until he sees Linda*) Right!
You — out here, now!
Carol She won't listen Eddy. (*Seeing Robbie in the corridor*) Hia
Robbie.

Eddy and Linda face-off

Robbie Eddy, come on — we can't go in there — it's the Ladies'.
Eddy Get outside, I said.
Carol I've told y' Eddy — she won't take notice of anyone.
Eddy (*beat*) All right. Okay. Stay where y' are. (*Moving into the Ladies'*)
I'll stay as well. (*To the other lads*) Get in here!

They can't

(*To Linda*) Doesn't bother me that it's the Ladies'. Rules? They mean
nothin' to me. (*To the lads*) I said get in here!

*In various states of reluctance and tortured embarrassment they do so —
each of them avoiding looking at anything and, in Billy's case entering
backwards and keeping his eyes fixed on the doorframe*

Robbie (*half whispered*) Eddy — This is the Ladies'!
Kav (*half whispered*) Eddy — we're in the womens' bogs!
Eddy Stay where y' are! What does it matter where it is? Y' don't
worry about names on doors — they don't bother me. I go where I
wanna go. (*Turning to Linda*) Now you listen to me! You might be
Dave's tart – yeh? But I am his mate! His best mate. Dave's our mate.
You might try an' treat him like shite but we don't.

Linda is holding and matching his gaze

Goin' round tellin' people that you're not marryin' him — you! Don't
you even think of treatin' a man like that — understand? You just
learn y'self a bit of respect an' loyalty. An' don't you go round tellin'
no one that you're not marryin' Dave. Because you are tomorrow!
Linda Piss off, little man! (*She quickly turns and goes into a cubicle,
closing the door behind her*)

*Eddy moves fast, banging open the door and grabbing Linda by the
arm*

Eddy Don't — just fuckin' don't — you! Now you listen to what I'm sayin' girl. You play awkward fuckers with me, you do it once more tonight an' I'll get that posin' bastard you've been dancin' with an' I'll break every finger he's got. Did you hear me, eh? He'll never play that fuckin' guitar again! We've already seen him. He's been warned. And so have you. Did you hear me?
Linda Yes. All right. Yes. okay...

He lets go of her but stays close

Eddy He's crap y' know. (*Beat*) He can't really play the guitar. Y' think he's good don't y'? Well he's not. (*Beat*) I know about guitars. I play the guitar. Chords I play. G and F an' D minor.
Robbie Come on Eddy — if we're seen in here...
Eddy You don't wanna be impressed by him girl. He's all show. I could've been in a group. A famous group. I play the guitar. (*To the women*) She's all right now. She's come to her senses. Haven't y' eh?
Linda (*totally impassive*) Yeh.
Kav Come on Eddy, this is the Ladies'.
Robbie Come on...
Eddy Right. (*To Linda*) See you in church!

Eddy, Robbie, Billy and Kav go to the Gents' where Eddy begins to run a basin of water

Come on let's get Dave sorted out. I've had enough of this place. We're goin' the club.

They begin to try and sober Dave up by dousing his head in water

Carol Eddy was right, wasn't he Linda?
Linda Yeh. Yeh.
Bernadette Oh Lind'... Linda... thank goodness you've come to your senses.
Frances I'm always tellin' y' about your moods, aren't I Lind'?

Maureen comes down the steps, heading for the Ladies'

Bernadette Well I'm just glad that it's all been sorted out...
Carol Ah yeh. (*Embracing Linda*) Come on now Linda eh? I didn't mean anythin' harsh that I might have said, y' know.

Maureen rushes in

Maureen What's happenin'?

Bernadette It's okay Mo. Everything's fine now.

Maureen Ah I'm glad. Hia Lind'. Now we can all go back to havin' another great time.

Bernadette Yeah! Come on — let's all get out there.

Maureen But 'ey, listen the group's not gonna be playin'.

Frances Why not?

Maureen I dunno. They just announced it. There's not enough power or somethin', for their equipment.

Bernadette 'Ey, I bet I could put a bit of power in their equipment, eh?

All but Linda dutifully laugh

Eh. Lind'?

Linda Yeh.

Frances What we gonna do now?

Carol Why don't we go somewhere else?

Frances What does Linda want to do?

Bernadette Linda only wanted to come here 'cos there was live music. If there isn't gonna be any she won't mind movin' on. Will y' Linda?

Carol Let's go to a proper club.

Maureen Ah shall we eh?

Bernadette Come on eh. Eh Lind'?

Linda If you like.

Carol I'll go get the coats. Hurry up. We'll get a taxi before the pubs start emptyin'.

Carol goes into the corridor and exits

The others start preparing to go

In the Gents'

Kav Come on Dave… Dave — we're goin' down the club — have another bevvy…

Billy We'll have to get in before eleven y' know.

The girls leave the loo and make their way up the stairs

Carol comes through with their coats

They begin preparing themselves to leave. Linda leans on the wall, slightly apart from the rest of them

In the Gents'

Eddy Sod it. Come on. Let's get him out. We'll get a taxi.

At the top of the steps

Frances I'll go see if there's any taxis passin'…

Frances exits through the street doors

Bernadette (*to Linda*) All right love?
Linda Feel a bit sick.
Bernadette (*to the others*) That'll be the nerves. Don't worry love, you'll be okay tomorrow. Be all right on the big day, won't y'?

Eddy, Robbie, Billy and Kav appear at the top of the stairs, carrying Dave

Linda… Close your eyes.

Linda does as ordered. Maureen crosses to her and turns her to face the wall

Maureen Turn this way Lind. Y' can't be too safe y' know. (*Getting a glance of Dave*) God, Linda — count y'self lucky y' can't see him. What a state.
Robbie All right girls.
Carol Hia Robbie.
Bernadette 'Ey — don't be bringin' him here. We don't want tomorrow's bride seein' tomorrow's groom.
Kav He can't see a bleedin' thing.
Robbie He's well away.
Carol Hia Robbie…
Robbie Here — put him down here till we get a cab — he'll be all right.

They lower Dave down, propping him against the wall. Robbie leaves the others to it and shoots across to Carol

'Ey, I was hopin' I'd get a dance with you tonight.
Carol Oh, were y'?
Robbie Who's er — lookin' after y'?
Carol No one.

Robbie No one? Y' mean no one's lookin' after a lovely little thing like you? (*Putting his arm around her*) We'll have t' do somethin' about that, won't we?

Frances enters

Frances There's no taxis anywhere.
Eddy (*clocking Robbie and Carol who are now well into each other*) I'll er, I'll go see if I can find one…
Bernadette Need a hand Eddy?
Eddy What? (*Quickly checking her out*) Yeh. All right then.

Eddy and Bernadette exit. Bernadette indicating her "success" to the others

Maureen beams a smile at Billy who doesn't know where to put himself. Kav approaches Robbie who is now necking with Carol

Kav Eh. Robbie — y' were only jokin', weren't y'?
Robbie (*interrupted*) What?
Kav Y' were only jokin'— about the clap? Weren't y'?
Robbie Yeh. (*Aside*) Fuck off will y'…
Kav What?
Robbie (*breaking again; indicating Frances who is stood alone*) Do one!

Kav moves across to Frances

Frances There's no taxis.
Kav I know. It's terrible, isn't it? Can't get one anywhere.
Frances Your name's Kav, isn't it?
Kav My real name's Tony. But they call me Kav.
Frances Oh.
Kav Hey.
Frances What?
Kav Come here.

She does

Frances What?
Kav Give us a kiss.
Frances Oh sod off!
Kav Come here.

He kisses her. She responds

Throughout the above, Maureen has been edging along the wall towards Billy and is now alongside him. He continues to try and ignore her

Maureen Hia.
Billy (*not looking*) Hello. (*He coughs*)
Maureen I see everyone's made friends!
Billy Yeh.
Maureen Has anyone ever told you, you've got "come to bed" eyes?
Billy I don't think so.
Maureen Well you have y' know.
Billy Have I? Oh.
Maureen Tch — you're a real smooth-talker you, aren't y'? (*She goes to walk away*)

Billy quickly grabs her and starts necking with her

Linda turns and opens her eyes. Looks at the scene before her. Looks at Dave. She crosses to him, bends down and un-noticed by the others, quietly shakes him

Linda (*quietly*) Open your eyes... Look at me — look at me... Open your eyes — come on — just look once... Come on. (*Shaking him*) Look at me!... (*Shaking him roughly*) I said look at me!
Carol Linda what are y' ——
Robbie Come here.
Carol But she's ——
Robbie I've told y' — he can't see nothin', he's well away... Come here...

They begin necking again
Linda Open your eyes an' look... Ye — that's it — that's it...

She holds his brief gaze before resting him back against the wall she stands and we hear the beginning of "Superstition" which goes on to underscore the subsequent action

Bernadette enters, linking arms with Eddy

Linda begins to walk down the steps to the toilets

Bernadette You all right Linda?

Linda Yeh. I'm fine, I'm just... I'm all right. You stay there. I'm just …
I think I'm gonna be sick.
Bernadette (*to Eddy*) Wait here. (*She starts down the steps after Linda*)
Linda (*in anger*) I said stay there!
Bernadette (*momentarily stopped by the vehemence of it*) Linda!

She starts to approach, Linda backing away down stairs

I'm only coming to look after you love. You don't wanna be all on
your own when y' sick.
Linda Don't come near me!
Bernadette (*moving down steps*) Now Linda don't start this…

*Linda goes to enter the Ladies'. Instead, she looks across the corridor,
rushes into the Gents'*

Linda! Are you out of y' mind — that's the Gents' — you've gone in
the Gents' — come out of there, come out.

*Unable to bring herself to follow Linda into the Gents, Bernadette rushes
back up the steps, shouting as she does so*

Eddy! Eddy… She's gone into the Gents' — Linda's gone into the —
an' I can't go in there, Eddy, Eddy — Linda's gone into the Gents'.
Eddy Well, what' d' y want me to do about it?
Bernadette (*beat*) Men! (*She turns and rushes back down the steps,
gingerly opening the door and peering inside*)

*Throughout the above, Linda is searching for a means of escape. She
tries the main window but it is reinforced glass. We see her open a
cubicle, which has a small window in the back wall. She comes out
looking for something with which she can smash open the window.
She sees the condom dispenser and smashes it off the wall. Taking the
dispenser into a cubicle, Linda, seeing Bernadette enter closes and bolts
the door*

Linda… Linda.

*She moves towards the cubicle and trying the door, finds it locked. She
tries to force the door – but can't*

Linda!

Hearing the first blow of the dispenser hitting the window, Bernadette realizes now, turns and rushes back up the steps, calling frantically as she does

Eddy! Eddy – she's tryin' to do a runner — Eddy.

Eddy, propelled into action, which is punctuated by the sound of the window being smashed, now legs it down the steps and following Bernadette into the Gents'

Eddy, quick, get it open — get that open.

Eddy shoulders the door until it finally gives. He sees the smashed window

Eddy Fuck!

Eddy turns and legs it back up the stairs as Bernadette jumps up onto the lavatory pan in order to see out of the window space. We hear the sound of a van engine bursting into life

Bernadette The van. Eddy — the van... She's getting' in that van! (*She suddenly loses her footing, which results in one leg slipping into the lavatory pan*)

Upstairs, Eddy goes running past everyone and out of the street doors

Kav (*prompted by Eddy running out*) 'Ey, come on... Eddy must have got a taxi.
Bernadette Linda!
Kav Come on there's a couple pullin' up...
Carol Taxis... quick, come on, the taxis are here.
Bernadette She's gone... She's gone.
Maureen (*to Bernadette who trudges, sop-footed up the stairs*) Berni... Berni — come on...
Carol Come on Berni — we're all goin' the club with the lads — the taxi's here.
Bernadette Where's Eddy?
Carol He must be in the taxi — come on — get Linda — come on...

Carol exits

Bernadette Carol, Carol hold on...

Bernadette exits

Shouting, from outside. It's garbled but as it dies away we hear Eddy

Eddy (*off*) Bastards... Come back... Bastards.

He enters, panting for breath

Bastards! (*Seeing Dave, walking down to him, and standing getting his breath back*) The bastards. They've bailed out on us Dave. They've left us. (*Going to sit by Dave*) They've all gone Dave. Linda, your Linda's gone. She's fucked off Dave. The bitch. Well, fuck 'em. Fuck them all. (*Lifting Dave towards the doors*) Well y've got no baggage weighin' y' down. There's nothin' holdin' us back now. We can go anywhere... Anywhere.

Eddy carries Dave out through the doors

Black-out

THE END

FURNITURE AND PROPERTY LIST

ACT I

On stage: *Ladies':*
WCs
Washbasin
Paper-towel dispenser
Waste-paper basket
Wall hand-dryer
Mirror
Make-up ledge
Chairs

Gents':
Urinals
WC. *In it:* toilet paper
Paper-towel dispenser
Waste-paper basket
Washbasin
Wall hand-dryer
Mirror
Condom dispenser

Off stage: Gear (**Roadie**)

Personal: **Girls**: handbags containing make-up, comb etc.
Linda: L-plates and bride-to-be attire
Kav: pencil
Maureen: a quarter bottle
Eddy: a quarter bottle of Scotch

ACT II

Off stage: Coats (**Carol**)

Personal: **Girls**: handbags as before
Robbie: felt-tipped pen

LIGHTING PLOT

Property fittings required: lights in corridor, Ladies and Gents

Interior. Ladies' and Gents' toilets, a corridor. The same scene throghout

ACT I	Evening	
To open:	Full general lighting in corridor, Ladies and Gents **NB** Corridor lights remain on throughout	
Cue 1	**Girls** enter *Fade lighting on Gents'*	(Page 1)
Cue 2	**Girls** sit waiting for **Linda** *Cross-fade to Gents'*	(Page 6)
Cue 3	**Boys** exit from corridor *Cross-fade to Ladies'*	(Page 15)
Cue 4	**Bernadette:** "Linda, Linda!" *Cross-fade to Gents'*	(Page 17)
Cue 5	**Eddy** produces a quarter bottle of Scotch *Cross-fade to Ladies'*	(Page 19)
Cue 6	**Linda** and **Frances** exit *Cross-fade to Gents'*	(Page 22)
Cue 7	**Eddy:** "I've just seen her now, out there — dancin'!" *Black-out*	(Page 30)
ACT II	Evening	
To open:	Lights in Ladies', corridor **NB** Corridor lights remain on throughout	
Cue 8	**Girls** go down corridor singing *Cross-fade to Gents'*	(Page 33)

EFFECTS PLOT

ACT I

ACT II